What's a Bank Worth?

Realistic valuations of the financial industry

Published in April 2012 by

Spiramus Press Ltd
102 Blandford Street
London W1U 8AG
Telephone +44 20 7224 0080
www.spiramus.com

ISBN 978 1907444 05 0

British Library Cataloguing-in-Publication Data.
A catalogue record for this book is available from the British Library.

Printed and bound in Great Britain by Good News Digital Print, part of the Berforts Group, Stevenage.

Contents

Table of figures

Acknowledgments

This book is not completely new, but is based upon "Valuing Banks in Uncertain Times". There are, however, a number of differences. The most substantial change is that this book does not have a specific section for Islamic financial institutions. Instead, it has a number of additional sections dealing with asset bubbles, financial regulations, risk management, and interest.

All errors are, of course, my own, but I would not have been able to get all the other parts right without some help. My sincere thanks go to Prof Simon Archer for his invaluable support during my research, which eventually led to the publication of "Valuing Banks in Uncertain Times".

To my dear friends Dr Julinda Nuri and Dr Edith Szivas for their support and comments. Further thanks go to Peter Goodman for his random thoughts (as one does) on Value at Risk and to Alison Swaisland for her assistance with obtaining the forecast data.

Finally to all my friends and family for their support in which ever shape or form. To anyone I may have forgotten to mention rest assured that your contribution was equally well valued.

Why Value?

The Industrial Revolution, globalisation and the segregation of ownership and control have all significantly strengthened the requirement to be able to place a value on a business. The question "Why Value?" is therefore not one that has only recently surfaced. The requirement to measure current and future (expected) profitability is a concept that has mainly developed over the last 250 years or so, but has been debated over the centuries, particularly in combination with the concepts of risk and return. As early as 1776 Adam Smith stated that:

> "The owner [of the capital], though discharged of all the labour, expects that his profits should bear a regular proportion to his capital. [...] The lowest rate of profit must be more than sufficient to compensate the losses to which the employment of stock is exposed. The lowest rate of interest must more than compensate the occasional losses to which lending is exposed."[1]

Smith clearly identified not only the need to measure profitability, but also recognised that risk and return are linked to one another in such a way that higher risks need to be offset by higher returns.

The ability to value a business will assist shareholders in their capacity as its owners in their investment decision-making process. In addition, being able to value a business is equally relevant to other stakeholders with an interest in the business such as employees, governments, regulators and suppliers.

The research study that forms the basis for this book shows that, over the period of the study, in excess of 80% of the share price of banks is explained by its fundamental value. Although what drives the other 20% is not clearly defined, it is at least in part associated with market sentiment and herd behaviour among investors. The market turmoil

---

[1] Smith, A. (1881) *An Inquiry into the Nature and Causes of the Wealth of Nations, Abridged version with notes and appendices by Wolsely P. Emerton, M.A. B.C.L.*, Oxford: James Thornton

that started off with the subprime loan debacle in the United States mid 2007 has had a significant impact on the economy, with banks being taken over and/or nationalised, and a significant drop in the value of all the major exchanges. As a result of large write downs, the resulting lack of liquidity in the market and, equally important, the loss of trust in the banking system, have drastically reduced lending practices which in turn has had a knock-on effect throughout the global economy. At the time of writing, we still have to see what the impact of the various rescue packages will be and how rapidly the economy will recover, and comparisons with the Great Depression of the late 1920s, early 1930s have already been made.

The current downturn begs the question whether the sharp decline in share prices implies that the value of the underlying companies has changed dramatically in a short space of time. Or is price maybe not the best benchmark to determine company value, given that price includes some type of psychological element? The answer probably lies somewhere in the middle and is unlikely to be easy, and although there are likely to be more questions than answers, interesting enough to pay at least some attention to.

We will start with a brief review of the theoretical framework surrounding the valuation of companies, and which model appears to be most suitable for firm valuation. The question that then arises is how banks differ and the impact of these exact differences on the valuation model. Is it possible to use the same model to value a bank? As will be shown, it is indeed possible although the components of the models will have to be determined carefully.

Islamic banks have additional challenges attached to them when it comes to valuation, such as the fact that transactions have to be based on an underlying asset or an enterprise. Valuation of Islamic banks is currently further hindered by, among others, a lack of data, relatively small bank size and the fact that they are mainly based in countries that are still classified as emerging markets. On the other hand, this does not mean they cannot be valued in a similar way. On the contrary, it is possible, albeit more challenging. A number of the issues facing Islamic bank valuation, however, are similar to newly started banks in similar jurisdictions.

The data used for the study that forms the basis of this book predates the global financial crisis of 2007/2008. Although current events do not by definition invalidate the results, they do raise a number of related questions such as how the model presented might hold up throughout an economic cycle and whether or not the asset bubble and subsequent bust could have been predicted.

The remainder of this book is divided into two main sections. The first part explores different types of valuation models and how the selected "residual income model" can be applied to the valuation of banks as well as to Islamic banks. The second part will focus on challenges which are not necessarily only applicable to banks and will consider issues such as the impact of the media on share prices, valuation in uncertain times and market sentiment.

WHY VALUE?

Part 1

The Theory of Determining Bank Value

1 Valuation of Firms

Ever since Adam Smith's *Wealth of Nations*, the desire to be able to measure current and estimated future profitability of a firm, both in isolation and in comparison to others operating in the same market segment, has intensified. In 1890, Alfred Marshall stated in volume 1 of the *Principles of Economics*[2]:

> *"What remains of his capital at the current rate may be called his Earnings of Undertaking or Management."*

Marshall's 'Earnings of Undertaking' are in fact identical to Economic Profit, which is calculated by subtracting a capital charge from net income after taxes. The 'Earnings of Undertaking' are based on current returns, and do not necessarily include future expected growth or the risk related to the (long-term) investment. Expected future growth and risk are, however, important issues for consideration. Any highly profitable investment is typically linked to a higher risk for the investor. Risk and future growth are further intertwined with current and future expected returns, capital and cost of capital.

1.1 Valuation Components

Regardless of which valuation model is used, the underlying components – risk, expected growth, estimated future returns, capital and cost of capital – will, in some shape or form, have to be incorporated. The estimation of each of these parameters is briefly described in the remainder of this section.

1.1.1 Growth

Growth most importantly concerns the growth that can be sustained by a firm over longer periods of time, typically for at least the next three to five years. In its most simplistic form, the sustainable growth rate can be determined by multiplying the earnings retention rate (which

---

[2] Marshall, A. (1895) *Principles of Economics*, 3rd Edition, London: Macmillan & Co 157

represents the proportion of income the firm retains for re-investment in the company) by the return on equity (ROE)[3]. The underlying assumptions when determining the growth rate are that a firm wants to grow as fast as possible, there is no requirement to issue new equity, and the firm wants to maintain its current capital structure and dividend policies. This raises an interesting issue during the current financial crisis, where particularly banks are receiving additional capital injections from their respective governments. This will be addressed in more detail in Part 2, Chapter 7 which reviews the potential impact of financial crises on valuation.

The main issue related to the determination of growth remains that the growth rate is generally based on historic data. However, history does not necessarily repeat itself.

1.1.2 Risk

In general, it can be stated that the return on an investment should reflect the level of risk incurred. In other words, an investor will only be willing to invest in a higher risk asset if he will have a reasonable chance of receiving a higher return reflecting this. The risk-return trade off in combination with his individual risk profile is one of the main motivators behind the investor's decision, at least, to consider an investment. The frontier on which, in equilibrium, all optimum, diversified portfolios are positioned is known as the Capital Market Line (CML) which was devised by Markowitz[4]. He developed the Expected Return – Variance (E-V) hypothesis based on the rules that an investor:

1. maximises discounted expected, or anticipated returns; and
2. considers expected return desirable and variance of return undesirable.

---

[3] The sustainable growth rate is typically calculated as follows: $g^* = (R)(ROE)$ where g^* represents sustainable growth, R is the Retention Ratio and ROE is the Return on Equity

[4] Markowitz, H. (1952) *Portfolio Selection*, The Journal of Finance, 12(1), 77-91

The CML represents the rates of return on efficient portfolios with different risk levels. It takes into account that an investor will always have some investments in the risk-free assets in his portfolio to mitigate some of the potential risk he takes with other investments. Whether or not an investment suits an individual investor will depend on his risk appetite and his optimum portfolio as measured by the CML.

1.1.3 Returns

> "Economists and accountants differ on the proper definition of profit. To the accountant, profit is the excess of revenues over expenses and taxes and is best measured by earnings. To the economist, earnings fail to include an important expense item, the opportunity cost of equity capital, contributed by the shareholders." Kimball[5]

This statement neatly defines why returns are difficult to measure – how to define a return depends very much on whom one is discussing the subject matter with.

Returns are, however, a major component in a valuation framework, and both current and future (expected) earnings need to be defined carefully. Different schools of thought exist when it comes to the identification of returns, the main ones being *earnings*, *free cash flow* and *dividends*, each with their own advantages and limitations.

The main limitations of *earnings* are associated with the use of realisation and matching principles in accounting which results in recognition of earnings in different periods than the underlying cash receipts and disbursements. *Free cash flow*, which addresses this issue, has its own disadvantages and neither *free cash flow* nor *earnings* incorporates how changes in future business conditions are expected to affect them. *Dividends* reflect the return to shareholders but do not represent the overall returns of the company. It could be argued that dividends are the only relevant valuation attribute since, ultimately,

---

[5] Kimball, R.C. (1998) *Economic Profit and Performance Measurement in Banking*, Boston: New England Economic Review, July/August, 35-53

only payoffs count and dividends alone can be consumed, but they have two main drawbacks. First, dividends paid reduce the actual market value of the company by the equivalent of the dividend payment, which can be observed as soon as a stock goes ex-dividend. Secondly, dividends have a negative impact on earnings in subsequent periods, mainly because the firm cannot reinvest dividends paid.

After all is said and done, *earnings* appear to be a superior measure when it comes to valuation, a standpoint which is neatly summarised below:

> "Even though accountants have not formally recognised the goal of having an earnings figure that measures value, they have done a remarkably good job of achieving this goal. That's the magic in earnings." Black[6]

This is further based on Black's findings that the Price/Earnings multiple is more stable than the Price-to-Book Value ratios, which leads to the conclusion that earnings as they are reported in the financial statements can be used directly when determining the value of a company.

The expected future value, which is discounted in the value of the company, can for exactly the same reason be based on the reported earnings figures, and the value of a firm can be defined as the current book value plus an infinite sum of discounted residual income or earnings over and above the required return on equity.

In order to predict estimated future returns with any degree of accuracy, the following key issues will need to be incorporated in the analysis[7]:

- **Micro-economics of the firm.**

  In general, structural Residual Income models have not attempted

[6] Black, F. (1980) *The Magic in Earnings, Economic Earnings versus Accounting Earnings,* Financial Analysts Journal, 36 (November/December), 19-24

[7] Walker, M. (1997) *Clean Surplus Accounting Models and Market-based Accounting Research: A Review*, Accounting and Business Research, 27(4), 341-355

to identify the main type of micro-economic shocks that impact upon residual income. Specifically, no reference is made to the distinction between demand and supply conditions, shocks that are specific to the individual accounting entity, and shocks that affect the entire industry.

- **Competitive Forces**

  Competitive interaction of the firm with firms in the same industry needs to be incorporated in the assessment of residual income since competitive forces eventually drive residual income towards a long run equilibrium level of zero. As a result of the working of competitive forces, the consensus among researchers and practitioners is that the rate of mean reversion is around 38% per year, meaning that any exceptional returns due to a competitive advantage will on average only last for a period of around three years. As a result, the majority view is that expected future returns should be determined using a two-stage approach. During the first stage of around three years, the growth rate of return is determined based on the expected growth of the individual firm. The second stage provides the terminal value, which attempts to capture the reversion of the firm's long-term returns to the industry average.

1.1.4 Capital

A firm's capital base consists of the total capital available to the firm to apply to the business and to generate a return. For any type of organisation, the total capital base consists of the following:

- Equity Capital which includes share capital and reserves;
- Long-term Debt such as long-term loans and bonds issued;
- Short-term Debt such as short-term working capital loans, bank overdrafts and revolving credits.

When applying the Miller Modigliani Theorem[8] it would not make a

[8] Miller and Modigliani (1961) showed that in perfect and complete capital markets, a firm's dividend policy does not affect its value. The basic premise of their

difference to the firm whether it finances itself with debt or equity. However, due to taxation, cost and leverage issues, firms typically make a calculated choice on how to structure their finances.

1.1.5 Cost of Capital

The cost of capital is generally defined as the opportunity cost of capital for the firm's existing assets[9]. In order to estimate the cost of capital, the different components of capital need to be considered. Owing to the fact that equity and debt capital have different characteristics, each demands a different required return. When making investment decisions, the firm will normally base itself on the total available capital, and not make the distinction between debt and equity components. Cost of capital is commonly expressed as the Weighted Average Cost of Capital (WACC) as in equation (1), which provides an approximation of the total cost of capital.

$$WACC = r_{Capital} = r_{Debt}\left(\frac{D}{(D+E)}\right) + r_{Equity}\left(\frac{E}{(D+E)}\right)$$

Equation 1 – Weighted Average Cost of Capital

where *r*: Required return (on capital, debt or equity)

E: Market value of Equity

D: Market value of Debt

---

argument is that firm value is determined by choosing optimal investments. The net payout is the difference between earnings and investment, and is simply a residual. Because the net payout comprises dividends and share issues/repurchases, a firm can adjust its dividends to any level with an offsetting change in shares outstanding. From the perspective of the investors, dividend policy is irrelevant, because any desired stream of payments can be replicated by appropriate purchases and sales of equity. Thus, investors will not pay a premium for any particular dividend policy. (Constantinides, G.M., Harris, M, Stulz, R.M, *Handbook of the Economics of Finance: Corporate Finance*, Amsterdam: Elsevier B.V.

9 Brealey, R.A., S.C. Myers and A.J. Marcus (2003) *Fundamentals of Corporate Finance*, International Edition, New York: McGraw-Hill, p 321

In order to enable international comparison, the cost of debt should be calculated on an after-tax basis, which results in the effective cost of debt being calculated as r_{debt}(1-tax rate).

Whilst the market value of equity of a listed company can be determined relatively easily based on the share price quoted in the financial markets, the perceived market value of unlisted debt might be more difficult to determine. Bond prices quoted in the financial markets for a company with the same characteristics and credit worthiness could be used as a benchmark or alternatively, the book value of debt can provide a reasonable approximation of the value of the debt. The interest rate of fixed-rate debt can then be used as an approximation for the required return on debt.

The cost of both debt and equity is not only based on market conditions, but also on the perceived risk of the investment. Hence, if WACC is estimated correctly, it can be used as an appropriate risk adjusted discount factor. For banks however, capital mainly consists of equity without any significant debt (see section 2.2.2). As a result, only the required return on equity is relevant to determine a bank's cost of capital.

1.2 The Models

There are two basic ways to look at the value of a business:

- Value created over a specific period of time. This consists of earnings (including dividends) over and above the cost of capital employed during the reporting period. This information is available in the company's periodic reporting and includes how the income is distributed.
- Value of a company at a particular point in time. This is a function of its current and future expected earnings, rate of return, capital and cost of capital. Where future expected earnings are concerned, the most important characteristic is whether they can be sustained and grow in combination with the risk taken to obtain them.

For a company that is not a going concern but likely to be terminated within a short period, the emphasis will be on the value created during the current period. For any going concern, both the value created during the current accounting period as well as the value at a particular point in time are relevant for the investment decision-making process. It is the value of a company at a particular point in time which is the main subject of this book. Although many different models have been applied to the valuation of companies, some are ultimately more suitable than others for many different reasons. The main criteria used here are the ease of use with publicly available information, the number of variables and, as far as possible, proven reliability. The most significant different models are detailed further below.

1.2.1 Discounted Cash Flow

Discounted Cash Flow (DCF) models determine the value of a company as the present value of all expected future cash distributions discounted at the opportunity cost of capital. The general arguments in favour of these models are that they are best positioned to value a company since the value of the company's equity, assuming the business is a going concern, arises from the company's capacity to generate cash flows for the equity shareholders.

Two main types of DCF model can be distinguished, the Dividend Growth Model (DGM) and the Free Cash Flow Model (FCF), which are both based on the discounting of an expected future cash flow at the required return.

Dividend Growth Model

The Dividend Growth model (DGM) uses the level of dividend, expected growth in dividends, and an appropriate discount rate to determine the value of the business, where generally explicit forecasts of dividend are used for the short-term forecasting period in combination with a Continuing Value for the going concern as represented in equation (2) below:

$$P_0 = \frac{Div_1}{(1+r)} + \frac{Div_2}{(1+r)^2} + \dots + \frac{Div_t}{(1+r)^t} + \frac{Div_{t+1}}{(r-g)(1+r)^t}$$

Equation 2 – Dividend Growth Model

where P_0: Price at time 0

Div: Dividend

r: Required return

g: Growth

The value of the firm is then calculated as the price (P_0) multiplied by the number of shares. The main disadvantage of this model is that it mainly considers the pay-out to equity investors and does not necessarily incorporate any future additional returns which may be achieved by reinvesting the profits in the firm and the opportunity for which will be lost by paying out dividends.

Free Cash Flow Model

This model is similar to the DGM represented in equation (2), but replaces the expected future dividend stream with the expected free cash flows to the firm, which are in turn discounted at the appropriate discount rate. Free cash flow represents the cash that a company is able to generate after laying out the funds required to maintain or expand its asset base. Free cash flows can be calculated as follows:

	Net Income
+	Amortisation/Depreciation
-	Changes in Working Capital
-	Capital Expenditures
=	**Free Cash Flow**

The main question arising in the context of Discounted Cash Flow models is which cash flow series (dividends or free cash flow) best represents the expected future earnings stream and thus the value of the firm. Neither provides a full picture. They do not incorporate how changes in future business conditions are expected to affect the future cash distributions and, in addition, the DGM does not take into consideration the advantages of retained earnings as a basis for growth.

Regardless of whether dividends or free cash flows are used, the main driver of these models is that the expected value of the firm is arrived at by discounting the expected cash flows at a benchmark which is represented by the firm's cost of capital.

1.2.2 Economic Profit

The main characteristic of Economic Profit models is that they calculate a periodic spread between the Rate of Return on Capital and the Cost of Capital. A variety of Economic Profit models exist, the main ones being Residual Income and Economic Value Added.

Residual Income Models

Residual Income in itself can be defined as earnings over and above the cost of capital, discounted at the required return on equity as detailed in equation (3)

$$RI_t = \left(Earnings_t - (r_e \times B_{t-1}^e)\right)$$

Equation 3 – Residual Income

The Residual Income valuation models[10] determine the value of a company as the value of invested capital plus the present value of the stream of differences between (accounting) earnings and a charge for the use of capital, discounted at the cost of capital, and can be defined as:

---

[10] Lee, C.M.C., J. Myers and B. Swaminathan (1999) *What is the Intrinsic Value of the Dow,* The Journal of Finance, 54(5), 1693-1741

Frankel, R. and M.C. Lee (1998) *Accounting Valuation, Market Expectation, and Cross-sectional Stock Returns,* Journal of Accounting and Economics, 25, 283-319

$$V_t^e = B_t^e + \sum_{i=t+1}^{\infty} \frac{E_t[RI_t]}{(1+r_e)^i}$$

Equation 4 – Basic Residual Income Valuation Model

Substituting Residual Income (RI) with its individual components then gives:

$$V_t^e = B_t^e + \sum_{i=t+1}^{\infty} \frac{E_t[Earnings_i - (r_e \times B_t^e)]}{(1+r_e)^i}$$

Equation 5 – Residual Income Valuation Model

Where B^e_t is book value of equity at time *t*, $E_t[..]$ is the expectation based on information available at time *t*, $Earnings_i$ are the Earnings for period *i*, B^e_i the book value of capital at the start of the period *i*, and r_e the required return on equity.

Equation (5) attempts to represent the consensus view which indicates that the value of a company is not based on a single notion of dividend, cash flows or earnings, but is a combination of current book value and future expected residual income, discounted at the cost of capital. This model is generally found to have a high predictive power, especially using longer specific forecasting periods.

Similar to the Dividend Discount models and Free Cash Flow models, the main disadvantage of the Residual Income model is related to the fact that it contains an element of expectation, which is generally classified as unobservable.

Economic Value Added

Economic Value Added (EVA) as developed and trademarked by Stern Stewart is based on the more general measure of Economic Profit, and is, in its simplest form, defined as follows:

$$EVA = (r - c^*) \times Capital$$

Equation 6 – Economic Value Added

where r represents the rate of return, and c^* the Weighted Average Cost of Capital.

EVA is based on the Residual Income model, where operating profits are reduced by a charge related to the use of capital. In further development of EVA, Stern Stewart identifies a total of 164 adjustments that are required in order to 'correctly' estimate net operating profits and capital. The underlying reason for these adjustments is to compensate for what Stewart identifies as shortcomings in the accounting approach. Although Stewart's objective is to create a superior valuation measure, it results in an unmanageable model since the data required is often not directly available on the balance sheet, income statement, or notes. Although some marginal evidence is found that EVA's amendments might be incrementally important, the difference does not appear to be economically significant, may suffer from size-bias, and that even adjusted for size, they do not adjust for events outside the control of management such as general market movements. In addition, there is hardly any evidence that suggests that companies with a high EVA outperform the market.

1.2.3 Which Model?

Identifying the most superior valuation model is complicated, mainly due to the fact that each of the individual models has its own advantages and disadvantages attached to it. Ultimately, it is generally accepted that if applied correctly, each of the models will provide exactly the same equity valuation. Even so, most research in the general area of valuation of firms concludes that the Residual Income model (also often referred to as economic profit model), the oldest and, both in theory and practice, the most tested type of model, still continues to provide the most accurate results when determining the value of a business. With the main advantages being that they can easily be applied using accounting data, require estimates for a smaller number of variables, and provide a better valuation measure than the others. This further enhances the practical use of the Residual Income model as a tool for financial analysis.

The main issues that will need to be addressed with the Residual Income model are:

1. **Forecasting the infinite time horizon**

   The Residual Income model asks for an infinite time horizon for forecasted earnings. However, earnings are considered to be mean reverting as a result of competitive forces, and to revert to zero after around three years, thus reducing the need to forecast specifically for a longer time period.

   The Continuing Value starts at the end of the finite, three year, forecasting period and is discounted back to time t=0, and can in its simplest form be represented as follows:

$$\frac{CV}{(1 + r_e)^i}$$

Equation 7 – Discounted Continuing Value

It is calculated for the going concern using the long-term expected growth rate as represented in the equation (8):

$$CV = \frac{RI_3 \times (1 + g)}{(r_e - g)}$$

Equation 8 – Continuing Value

where *g* represents the expected long term growth rate.

2. **Subjective expectation**

   Forecasts may contain an unobservable element of subjective expectation. Using I/B/E/S consensus forecasts instead of individual estimates will reduce the subjective element.

   Frankel and Lee[11] researched the use of the I/B/E/S consensus

[11] Frankel, R. and M.C. Lee (1998) *Accounting Valuation, Market Expectation, and*

earnings forecasts as a proxy for market expectations of future earnings, and found that the resulting estimate of firm fundamental value has a high predictive power and reduces the subjective element of expectation.

Box 1 - Why use I/B/E/S forecasting data

Although not the only company collecting data, I/B/E/S, (the abbreviation of Institutional Brokers' Estimated System), is well regarded among academics, researchers and practitioners alike and is deemed to provide consistent high quality earnings data. A view which is shared, among others, by William Sharpe.[12] Not bad as far as recommendations go. Detailed and consensus estimates for up to 26 components including pro-forma EPS, revenue/sales and net income are collected for over 45,000 companies worldwide with history going back as far as 1976 for US Data and 1987 for international data. Data is provided by around 1,200 contributors. The consensus forecast is based on the consensus found between all the contributors.

The final model, including the Continuing Value component reads as follows:

$$V_t^e = B_t^e + \sum_{i=t+1}^{3} \frac{E_t[Earnings_i - (r_e \times B_t^e)]}{(1+r_e)^i} + \left(\frac{RI_3 \times (1+g) \Big/ (r_e - g)}{(1+r_e)^3} \right)$$

Equation 9 – Residual Income Valuation Model

In the model, three future earnings estimates are required beyond current earnings which, in the event of an equity valuation model as detailed in equation (9) can be determined on a per share basis. Each of

---

Cross-sectional Stock Returns, Journal of Accounting and Economics, 25, 283-319

[12] Stanford professor of finance, pioneer of the Capital Asset Pricing Model (see 2.2.3.1 below), and awarded Nobel Prize for Economics.

the estimates can be derived using the I/B/E/S consensus Earnings per Share (EPS) and estimates for the next periods, which are labelled F1MN and F2MN. Year-end book values are dependent on the current year Return on Equity or Earnings, and a sequential process is used to estimate future values.

Box 2 – Estimating Forecasted Earnings

Forecasted Earnings per Share for the first forecasting period are computed as the year 1 consensus forecast, divided by the average book value per share during the period t-1. Use of the average book value rather than year-end reduces the chances of extreme outliers, either positive or negative.

$$\text{Forecasted earnings}_t = F1MN/[(B_{t-1} + B_{t-2})/2]$$

For the second forecasting period, the Forecasted Earnings are calculated based on the two-year consensus forecast (F2MN) in accordance with the following equation:

$$\text{Forecasted earnings}_{t+1} = F2MN/[(B_t + B_{t-1})/2]$$

For the Continuing Value component, the Forecasted Earnings are calculated based on the two-year consensus forecast (F2MN) and the long term consensus forecast (LTMN) in accordance with the following equation:

$$FROE_{t+2} = [F2MN(1 + LTMN)]/[(B_{t+1} + B_t)/2]$$

The key to ensuring that the model provides an accurate valuation of a bank lies in the correct estimation of the individual parameters.

2 Why is Bank Valuation so Difficult?

> "Banks remain among the most difficult companies to value despite the multitude of regulatory and reporting requirements imposed on them. It is hard to determine the quality of their loan portfolio, to figure out what percentage of their accounting profits results from interest-rate mismatch gains, and to understand which business units are creating or destroying value."
>
> Copeland, Koller and Murrin[13]

What is it that makes any researcher and econometrician, as well as the majority of practitioners, run a mile when it comes to valuing a bank? Why are they deemed so much more difficult to value than any other company? Is it the sheer size of some of them or does it have something to do with general understanding of the industry? Or is it maybe mainly because of the fact that, even though banks produce their annual statement of accounts in line with accounting standards and provide a significant amount of information in the body of the annual accounts, we are still not really clear how they make their money? Transparency (or the lack of it) when it comes to off-balance sheet instruments, combined with the fact that banks are subject to a different set of risks we may not necessarily understand, and the increasing complexity of some of the relatively new products do not help either.

But does this mean we should just forget about valuing banks because the task is too difficult? Granted, the mess that the industry got itself in and that unfolded in late 2008 does not make attempting to value banks more attractive. On the other hand, one issue that is becoming clear from the 2008 credit crisis is that the market does not just trade on what it knows. Trading appears susceptible to herd behaviour and

---

[13] Copeland, T.E, T. Koller and J. Murrin (2000) *Valuation: Measuring and Managing the Value of Companies*, 3rd Edition, New York: John Wiley & Sons (p. 437 – 438)

(over-)reaction to news, both actual and expected.

The majority of market participants will agree that the ability to have a reasonable estimate of the value of any corporation is important to the working of the market, which would include the financial industry. Even though some of the parameters are estimated in a different way and a range of different types of risk need to be considered, the underlying model remains the same.

2.1 Bank Valuation Model

Valuing banks might be difficult, but is by no means impossible. Unlike other companies, banks' assets do not consist of plant, machinery or goods. In the same vein, banks' liabilities consist largely of deposits, which will need to be repaid, but are not the same as loans. Liability management, and the subsequent potential to create value, is part of the operational activities of the bank. Hence, any form of capital which is not equity, should not be considered as purely financing in the same way as debt financing is part of the funding of a company. As a result, valuation of a bank should be based on the Residual Income model for equity valuation as represented in equation (10)

$$V_t^e = B_t^e + \sum_{i=t+1}^{\infty} \frac{E_t[Earnings_i - (r_e \times B_t^e)]}{(1+r_e)^i}$$

Equation 10 – Residual Income Valuation Model

In this model, the required return on equity capital (r_e) is assumed to remain the same for the going concern, and will not change over the lifetime of the bank. In order to overcome the issue of having to forecast for an infinite time horizon, a continuing value will be introduced after three years of specific forecasting. This captures the fact that after three years:

- forecasting becomes increasingly difficult;
- the introduction of forecasting errors is likely; and
- the long-term residual income reverts to the industry mean.

The Continuing Value will be calculated for the going concern, using the long-term expected growth rate at the end of year three:

$$V_t^e = B_t^e + \sum_{i=t+1}^{3} \frac{E_t[Earnings_i - (r_e \times B_t^e)]}{(1+r_e)^i} + \left(\frac{RI_3 \times (1+g) / (r_e - g)}{(1+r_e)^3} \right)$$

Equation 11 – Residual Income Valuation Model

The assumptions underlying this model are that systematic risk levels as well as the riskless rate of return are assumed to remain constant over time for the going concern (represented by the Continuing Value), unless significant changes are expected in the perceived risk levels of the bank. In an equity valuation model, the value can be determined on a per share basis, in which case the earnings are determined on a per share basis. The value of the bank as a whole is then equal to the value per share multiplied by the number of shares outstanding. In the event of a per share valuation, the earnings in equation (11) can be replaced by Earnings per Share.

The key to the accuracy of the model's result lies in the correct application of the individual parameters as detailed in the next section.

2.2 The Parameters

Although the model only asks for a few parameters, it is important that these are estimated correctly. This will ensure that the value that is the result of the model is accurate. Each of the parameters required is detailed in this section.

2.2.1 Return

Off-balance sheet instruments such as guarantees, derivatives and letters of credit generate a significant part of the returns of banks, and the expected returns related to those as well as on-balance sheet items need to be considered when determining the total return of a bank.

Although the potential liabilities associated with the off-balance sheet instruments are not typically recorded in the financial statement, the earnings reported by the bank as reported on the income statement generally include all realised and unrealised earnings, be they generated by on- or off-balance sheet instruments.

In order to establish potential future returns for an individual entity, notes to the financial statements need to be analysed carefully, and competitive advantage will need to be taken into consideration when determining the sustainability of these earnings. Applying I/B/E/S consensus forecasts for the future estimated earnings ensures a rigorous analysis will already have taken place. In addition, applying a consensus forecast will reduce any subjectivity which is naturally present in estimations.

2.2.2 Capital

For any type of organisation, the total capital base consists of the following:

- Equity Capital;
- Long-term Debt;
- Short-term Debt.

Besides equity and debt, banks further have the funds of current and deposit account holders at their disposal and these are used to finance loan and investment operations. Although this implies that the bank's customers can be major liability holders, these funds are not considered part of the capital base of a bank, but should rather be viewed as what they are, the source used to fund their operations.

This also holds for venture capitalists and investment banks, where all or part of the invested funds are managed at the investor's (the client's) own risk, like discretionary portfolios and mutual fund investments. The funds are invested on behalf of the client, with the bank generating revenue from the investment service they provide. These funds are considered to be part of the liability management of the bank, but do not form part of the bank's capital base, which consists solely of equity capital. Like corporate debt, the cost of attracting deposits is based on the perceived risk a depositor is taking, which will be reflected in the overall net earnings.

Subordinated debt can be viewed in a similar way, with the possible exception of subordinated debt specifically issued to meet capital requirements. Subordinated debt issued as a pure source of funds can be considered as operational and hence should be excluded from capital, and the related costs will be deducted in the calculation of earnings. In contrast, subordinated debt issued to meet capital requirements could be considered for inclusion in the capital of the bank. However, the announcement by Deutsche Bank in early 2009 that they would not refinance their subordinated debt but instead pay the higher cost to service the debt under the existing agreement, supports the conclusion that even subordinated debt intended to meet capital requirements is part of the banks operational funding. In addition, it might be difficult, if not impossible to distinguish between these types of subordinated debt. For this study subordinated debt is considered as operational and not as part of capital.

2.2.3 Cost of Capital

The ability to measure the value of a firm on a stand-alone basis provides an indication of the overall value, but remains a relative concept as long as there is no comparison to other companies in the same industry or market place. One of the main benchmarks in valuation is the cost of capital of a firm in relation to the cost of capital of the market portfolio as a whole. Because a bank's capital constitutes solely of equity, there is no requirement to determine the Weighted Average Cost of Capital. Instead, the cost of equity, which is defined by the required return on equity, suffices. The main models to determine the required return on equity, namely the Capital Asset Pricing Model (CAPM) and the Arbitrage Pricing Theory (APT) are reviewed in further detail.

2.2.3.1 Capital Asset Pricing Model

The Capital Asset Pricing Model (CAPM) is developed based on Markowitz's[14] expected return – variance (E-V) hypothesis which is based on the rules that an investor (i) maximises discounted expected, or anticipated, returns and (ii) considers expected return desirable and variance of return undesirable. Markowitz then identified the Capital Market Line (CML), an efficient frontier on which, in equilibrium, all optimum, diversified portfolios are positioned. CAPM is defined as a utility function of investor preferences and replaces the Capital Market Line with the Security Market Line (SML), which is a graphical representation of the CAPM benchmark. CAPM has the following underlying assumptions:

- Investors have homogenous expectations regarding the possibilities of various end-of-period values for all assets;
- Common probability distribution describing the possible returns on the available assets is joint normal (i.e. they are both individually and in combination normally distributed);
- Investors choose portfolios that maximise their expected end-of-period utility of wealth;
- Investors may take long or short positions of any size in any asset, including the riskless asset.

CAPM is represented in the following equation:

$$r_e = r_f + \beta(r_m - r_f)$$

Equation 12 – Capital Asset Pricing Model

where r_e is the expected return on the security, r_f represents the risk-free rate represented by Treasury Bills or other government paper, r_m is

---

[14] Markowitz, H. (1952) Portfolio Selection, The Journal of Finance, 12(1), 77-91

the market rate of return and β (beta) indicates the systematic, undiversifiable risk of the investment in comparison with the market. It measures the correlation between an investment's value and movements in the overall market applying the following equation:

$$\beta_j = \frac{\delta_j}{\delta_m}\left(Corr(j,m)\right)$$

Equation 13 – The Calculation of β

In equation 13, *j* represents the return on an individual equity with *m* representing the return on the overall market. The resulting β defines the standard deviation of an individual asset relative to the standard deviation of the market, multiplied by the correlation co-efficient between the return on the risky asset *j* and the market *m*. For the market as a whole, β equals 1.0.

A high β implies that the stock price is more volatile than the average market, i.e. it goes up more than the average market price when prices are going up and goes down more than the average market price when the average prices are going down. A β close to 0 implies that the stock price is relatively unaffected by swings in the overall market.

2.2.3.2 Arbitrage Pricing Theory

The Arbitrage Pricing Theory (APT) is a multifactor asset-pricing model which expands CAPM with additional factors, and measures the sensitivity of an asset's returns to each additional factor with an individual factor-β. APT is based on the notion that besides the riskless rate and the systematic risk determined by CAPM, there is more than one other factor that systematically affects the returns of the market or an individual equity.

A variety of different additional factors can be considered for inclusion such as company size, book-to-market value and a company-specific risk premium. The main issue with a multifactor asset-pricing model is which factors to incorporate, and which factors to ignore. It is possible to incorporate factors that do not have any inherent explanatory value themselves, but are included solely because they fit the data presented. Furthermore, there is a risk that an additional factor added to the model may adversely affect the explanatory value of other factors.

The following factors are most generally used in the APT:

1. Industrial production index;
2. Short-term real rate;
3. Short-term inflation;
4. Long-term inflation;
5. Default risk.

With the resulting model being:

$$r_e = r_f + \beta_1\left(r(f)_1 - r_f\right) + \beta_2\left(r(f)_2 - r_f\right) + \ldots + \beta_n\left(r(f)_n - r_f\right)$$

Equation 14 – Arbitrage Pricing Theory

where $r(f)_n$ represents the expected rate of return on the market portfolio in relation to the nth factor, which is independent of all other factors, and β_n represents the sensitivity of the stock return to this factor.

Although there is some evidence that additional factors are relevant in the calculation of the cost of capital, it is generally found that this is not significant and certainly not off-set by the effort of collecting the additional information or the potential risk of introducing additional forecasting errors. Multifactor models may lead researchers to search the data for variables that describe the cross-section of average returns with hindsight and have no predictive power (i.e. data mining or data snooping).

2.2.3.3 CAPM or APT?

Rejection or acceptance of both CAPM and APT are never clean, and there is always a possibility that rejection of CAPM is due to an incorrect proxy for the market portfolio and the resulting poor estimates of the market. Company size and book-to-market value of equity appear to have some explanatory power over and above the market, which provides a reason to suggest that the multifactor asset-pricing model is better situated to provide a benchmark than CAPM.

Even though both CAPM and APT have disadvantages, they are still the most widely accepted models to determine the risk level of an asset or company in relation to the overall market portfolio. The relative simplicity of CAPM, combined with the fact that incorrect choices of factors may easily invalidate the APT, make CAPM the most useful model to determine the required return on equity.

2.2.4 Risk

Banks are subject to different risks from those faced by other types of firms as a direct result of the type of business they are in (see table 1). Some risks equally exist in other types of firms such as business and liquidity risk, whereas others such as market and interest rate risk are specific to banks. In order to quantify these risks, banks apply a measure known as Value at Risk (VaR) which attempts to measure the downside risk in one single number, taking into account financial leverage and diversification effects. The result of the VaR equation represents the maximum amount a bank is likely to stand to lose on a given day or over a number of days generally with a confidence interval of 95 or 99%. From a bank valuation perspective, any risk taken by the bank will have to be evaluated against the risk management framework in place and the cost of the measures.

Type of Risk	Description
Liquidity Risk	The risk of insufficient liquidity for normal operating requirements also defined as the ability of the bank to meet its liabilities when they fall due.
Interest Rate Risk	The risk arising from interest rate mismatches in volume, maturity and type (fixed vs. floating) of interest-sensitive assets, liabilities and off-balance sheet items.
Credit Risk	The risk that an asset or a loan becomes irrecoverable in the case of outright default, or the risk of delay in the servicing of the loan.
Settlement or Counterparty Risk	The risk that occurs if one party to a transaction pays funds or delivers assets prior to receiving its own funds or assets, hence exposing it to a potential loss.
Price Risk	The risk that the market price of an instrument traded in a well-defined market will be volatile. Market risk occurs in relation to debt securities, derivatives, equity derivatives and currency transactions held by a bank.
Leverage Risk (Capital Adequacy)	The risk related to the extent to which the assets of a bank may decline before the positions of its depositors and other creditors are jeopardised.
Event or Operational Risk	The risk of certain events occurring, e.g. disaster, regulatory or political events, or the (temporary) unavailability of IT systems.
Business Risk	The risks related to products, macro-economic cycles and technology changes.

Table 1: Types of Risks for Banks

2.3 The Proof

The value of any company, banks and non-banks alike, is the cumulative result of its financial performance, and the question that remains is whether or not the model actually works with real data. Residual Income models have two different functions, to evaluate periodic performance and to determine the value of a company at a certain point in time, and it is the second purpose that is tested here. The model itself has been tested extensively on a variety of industries, but always excluding financial institutions. In order to determine whether the results are valid, they will have to be tested against a benchmark. Frankel and Lee[15] have found that the V^e_t estimates of this model using I/B/E/S consensus forecasts are highly correlated with stock prices, which will be used as the benchmark here to show whether the model works.

The assumptions underlying the model are that systematic risk levels as well as the riskless rate of return are assumed to remain constant over time for the going concern (represented by the Continuing Value), unless significant changes are expected in the perceived risk levels of the bank. As a result, the forecast earnings are estimated based on the I/B/E/S consensus forecasts as defined in section 1.2.3.

The rest of this chapter details at a high level the data, statistical methods and results of the research. The detail displayed here is deliberately kept at a reasonably high level in order to ensure that a wider audience can be reached. Full details of the research including the definition of the hypothesis, full statistical methods and results of the various analyses are available from the URL below.[16]

---

[15] Frankel, R. and M.C. Lee (1998) *Accounting Valuation, Market Expectation, and Cross-sectional Stock Returns*, Journal of Accounting and Economics, 25, 283-319

[16] http://epubs.surrey.ac.uk/view/creators/Schoon=3ANatalie=3A=3A.html.

2.3.1 Data

Although Residual Income models have been empirically tested for non-financial institutions, this has not yet been done for banks. The Residual Income model for banks represented in equation (15) which is repeated below is used to determine the value of a bank at a specific period in time.

$$V_t^e = B_t^e + \sum_{i=t+1}^{3} \frac{E_t[Earnings_i - (r_e \times B_t^e)]}{(1+r_e)^i} + \left(\frac{RI_3 \times (1+g) / (r_e - g)}{(1+r_e)^3} \right)$$

Equation 15 – Residual Income Valuation Model

The model consists of four parameters for which estimations are required, being the book value of equity at time *t* (B^e_t), earnings, cost of capital (r_e), and the long-term growth rate (g). Capital is a function of the model and is equal to the book value of equity at the end of the year preceding the current forecasting period.

The current Book Value of equity is represented by the book value of owners' equity, as reported on the balance sheet, with the other parameters determined as defined in section 2.2. The data for the research underpinning this section is obtained from Datastream and spans the period 1991 to 2002.

The total available sample is used in two ways, and consists of banks listed on stock exchanges in markets that are considered information efficient such as *EURONEXT*, *LSE*, and *NYSE*. The dataset for this study is constructed based on the following criteria:

1. A minimum of five and a maximum of ten years of historical data are available for each of the banks in the population.
2. Only those institutions that have a listing for their banking activities are included. Combined bank and insurance companies that have a single listing covering both banking and insurance activities are

excluded from the dataset.

3. All observations are taken at the same annual interval to facilitate panel data analysis.
4. Only banks located in the United States of America and Western Europe are included in the sample. Banks in Japan are not included since no financial data for Japanese banks were available in Datastream.

In order to determine how the model best captures the market-based returns, an estimation sample and a control sample are constructed. The sample provides a realistic representation of the banking universe, and the bias to a particular geographical area or size is minimised.

From the original 1,718 banks in the sample, mainly for banks outside the US, the required data from Datastream (e.g. prices, financial information) are not available or incomplete. As a result, the remaining number of banks in the sample is 194, with a total number of 1,677 observations. Banks that are part of the total population are, for instance, HSBC, ABN AMRO Bank, Citigroup, Deutsche Bank, Bank of America, and Barclays. All data including the I/B/E/S consensus forecasts for each of the elements in the sample are obtained from Datastream on a per share basis. Due to the fact that the book value and price *per share* are used, any merger or acquisition activity in the period should not have a significant impact either on the value, or on the regression itself. Although this may vary from bank to bank, the total effect is deemed to cancel out over time, and the development of price and calculated value are considered to follow the same pattern. For any banks that have gone through a merger and/or acquisition, no data are available from Datastream for the original underlying entities. Royal Bank of Scotland for example, took over National Westminster in 2000. This can be seen from the development of both the price and the value estimation, as reproduced in table 2 below (Total assets in USD millions, both estimated value and year-end price are represented per share):

Item	1998	1999	2000	2001	2002
Total Assets	129,721	139,958	462,039	521,810	648,548
Estimated Value	4.79	6.50	10.96	17.00	14.79
Year-end Price	15.28	16.04	23.71	24.06	23.47

Table 2: Example – Royal Bank of Scotland

Both price and estimated value develop in the same way, and the data are included in the sample unadjusted, specifically since total assets and capital have developed along similar lines. This may, however, result in more extreme residual values in the regression model.

From the data items contained in Datastream, those listed in table 3 below have been used to calculate the value of a bank:

Data Item	Description
190	Dividend per share. Used to determine plough-back rate and the related effect on the future book values.
305	Equity Capital and Reserves. Used in combination with number of shares (NOSH) to determine Book value per share in the event item 1308 is not available.
625	Earned for ordinary. Net profit arrived at after deducting tax, minority interest and preference dividends, but before any reported extraordinary items and allocation to reserves.
1308	Book value per share
NOSH	Number of shares
F1MN	I/B/E/S consensus growth forecast, 1 year forward. Earnings per share
F2MN	I/B/E/S consensus growth forecast, 2 years forward
LTMN	I/B/E/S consensus long-term growth expectation. If not available, the value calculated in $FROE_{t+1}$ is used to proxy for $FROE_{t+2}$
392	Total Assets
Beta	Annual average of monthly Betas provided by Datastream. The monthly Betas are based on daily data.
Risk-free rate (R_f)	Where available government bond rates as available from Datastream are used. In all other cases, Worldscope MSCI data is used, which is only available from 1995 onwards.
Market rate (R_m)	Market rates are obtained from Datastream, calculated as the difference between time t and time t-1. The main index in a country is used as the basis to determine R_m
Price	The market price at fiscal year-end.

Table 3: Datastream Data Items

All amounts are in USD *per share*, which are automatically provided by Datastream. The exchange rates used are those at the time of the observation.

With the exception of Price, the data elements mentioned in table 3 are used to determine V^e_t using equation (15) (on page 30 above) for which both time series analysis and cross sectional analysis were applied using panel data, with a desired confidence level of 95%.

2.3.2 Statistical Method

The data for the 194 banks was analysed using two sub-sets of data, randomly generated from the original sample, which contained an equal number of observations (for full details of the analysis see the study referred to in footnote 16). A sample regression function[17] was used in which the independent variable is the equity value of the firm calculated using the Residual Income model and there is only one dependent variable being the total market capitalisation of the bank (i.e. price multiplied by the number of shares). The values resulting from the Residual Income model in itself should be sufficient to explain the cross-sectional variations in total market value, and hence no additional explanatory variables, such as firm size, are included. The Sample Regression Function is determined using the Ordinary Least Squares (OLS) method. The OLS is a technique used to define the best fit of the Sample Regression Function in such a way that the sum of the sample residuals is as small as possible. The data is analysed using time series and cross-sectional analysis.

Data varies from sample to sample and as a result, estimates will change. It is therefore necessary to be able to measure the 'reliability' or precision of the estimate. The precision of the regression model is determined by what is known as its standard error (s_e), with the goodness of fit being determined by R^2. R^2 measures the proportion of the total variation in the dependent variable (Y) explained by the regression model.

---

[17] The Sample Regression Function (SRF) is determined based on the Population Regression Function which is defined as $Y = \beta_1 + \beta_2 X + \mu$ where X is the independent or explanatory variable representing V^e_t, and Y is the dependent variable represented by the total market value, which equals the market price multiplied by the number of shares

2.3.3 Sample Details

Based on the criteria detailed in section 2.3.1, the total number of banks in the sample is 194 with a sufficient number of data points. Any bank with less than five years of calculated values has been excluded from the sample to enhance the accuracy of the results of the statistical tests. The resulting sample consists of banks from the United States and Western Europe, with in excess of 60% of the banks being based in the US (see box 3 on page 36).

Although the sample is significantly smaller than the total population, its geographical distribution mimics the geographical distribution of the banks in the full sample which contained all banks listed on the stock exchanges in the US and Europe.

As a result of the fact that data are no longer maintained for banks that have been are merged or have gone out of business, the sample suffers from what is known as survivorship bias[18]. Unfortunately, there is not much that can be done about this since data are often no longer available from an easily accessible source.

Besides the survivorship bias that occurs, the sample is prone to the occurrence of outliers in the analysis which is the result of the variety in balance sheet size and markets in which the banks operate (e.g. national versus internationally active). This is a common problem when applying cross-sectional data analysis since it deals with all members of the population at a given point in time, and all of the banks are different in size. This results in the occurrence of what is known as heteroskedasticity[19] which is controlled for using the White

---

[18] The tendency for failed companies to be excluded from performance studies due to the fact that they no longer exist. Survivorship bias causes the results of some studies to skew higher because only companies which were successful enough to survive until the end of the period are included. Similarly, mutual fund performance may be misleading due to survivorship bias if the fund family tends to merge or discontinue underperforming funds. (www.investorwords.com).

[19] In statistics, when the standard deviations of a variable, monitored over a specific amount of time, are non-constant. Heteroskedasticity often arises in two forms,

Heteroskedasticity Consistent Covariance.

Box 3 – Geographical distribution of the sample

Country	Banks	%
Belgium	3	1.5
Denmark	4	2.1
Finland	2	1.0
France	3	1.5
Germany	6	3.1
Greece	1	0.5
Ireland	2	1.0
Italy	10	5.2
Norway	9	4.6
Portugal	2	1.0
Spain	8	4.1
Sweden	2	1.0
Switzerland	9	4.6
Netherlands	2	1.0
UK	7	3.6
US	124	63.9

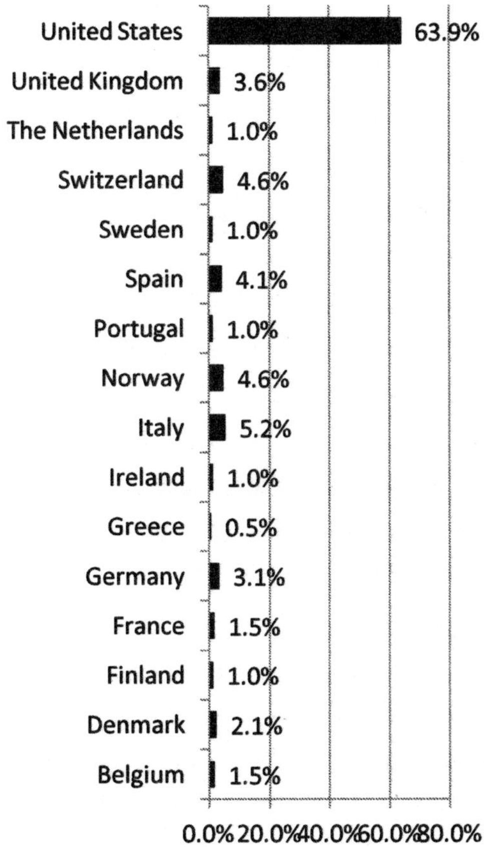

---

conditional and unconditional. Conditional heteroskedasticity identifies non-constant volatility when future periods of high and low volatility cannot be identified. Unconditional heteroskedasticity is used when futures periods of high and low volatility can be identified (www.investopedia.com).

Box 4 – Amendments for missing data elements

In a few instances not all data was available. Any amendments have been made in line with other research in the general area of equity valuation as follows:

- Where earnings are negative, 1% of total assets is used as a proxy. This percentage is determined based on the average earnings of banks over the period of this study.
- Where book value per share is not provided by Datastream, it is calculated by dividing equity capital and reserves by the number of shares.
- Where the consensus forecast for the long-term growth rate is not available, $FROE_{t+1}$ is used as a proxy for $FROE_{t+2}$.
- Observations for which no Market and/or Risk-free rate of return is available have been removed.
- Observations for which no Beta is available for individual banks have been removed.

In order to apply a time series analysis, the number of observations should be as high as possible. The dataset for the analysis applied to this research has ten observations per bank for the following reasons:

- The impact of mergers and acquisitions in the industry is significantly larger when applying a longer period;
- The model calls for annual data, and data is not always available for periods in excess of ten years;
- The results of the model are not only used to identify whether the model is applicable to banks in general, but also to assess whether it can be applied to Islamic banks. For Islamic banks, only a limited history is available. This is described in Chapter 3.

Inherent in the nature of the Residual Income models is the occurrence of first-degree serial autocorrelation, which results from the fact that the value of a bank (V^e_t) is based on the book value in the previous period. First-degree serial autocorrelation is controlled for within the sample.

2.3.4 Test Results

The different test results lead to the conclusion that the Residual Income can, to a significant degree, capture the cross-sectional differences in stock market value of banks over a significant period of time. The value calculated using the Residual Income model is highly correlated to market value and as such, the Residual Income model defined in this book and which is reproduced below, can be used to estimate the value of a bank.

Analysing the data purely on a cross-sectional basis, the results on a year-to-year basis, using the Ordinary Least Squares method[20], are as represented in table 4 below:

Year	Observations	Goodness of fit
1993	118	91%
1994	125	98%
1995	140	98%
1996	155	98%
1997	171	95%
1998	194	95%
1999	194	90%
2000	194	89%
2001	194	96%
2002	194	84%

Table 4: Cross-sectional Analysis Results

[20] The Ordinary Least Squares Method defines the best fit of the regression line in such a way that the sum of the sample residuals is as small as possible. For further detail on this statistical method see:

Thomas, J.J. (1983) *An Introduction to Statistical Analysis for Economists,* London: London School of Economics Handbooks in Economic Analysis, Second edition;

Gujarati, D.N. (2002) *Basic Econometrics,* 4th Edition, New York: McGraw-Hill International Editions

Although the values in the goodness of fit of the model (also known as R^2) differ between the years, these differences are not very significant and can largely be explained by market dynamics and overreaction to market shocks in the years 1999 (Asia), 2000 (Russian Rouble) and 2002 (Dot Com).

2.4 Valuing Banks – The Conclusion

> "Stock market behaviour is driven by investor sentiment as well as by clear-thinking rationality, and speculative action can drive market values away from fundamentals, and thereby away from the 'theoretically correct' estimation given by the valuation model." Barker[21]

After all is said and done, the conclusion based on the evidence presented will have to be that, as long as the parameters are estimated correctly and the right model is applied, it is ultimately possible to estimate the value of a bank in the same way as any other type of company. It is noteworthy that the results show the impact of bubbles and the reaction of market participants to associated news which manifests itself as a deterioration in the goodness of fit between the price and the estimated value determined using the Residual Income model.

---

[21] Barker, R. (2001) *Determining Value – Valuation Models and Financial Statements*, Harlow: Pearson Education Limited (6)

3 Further Observations

Numerous studies have identified the Residual Income model, outlined in the previous chapters, to work as a viable valuation approach for non-banks using stock-market valuations as a benchmark. Each of these studies has specifically excluded financial institutions. However, as the results in the previous chapters show, it is indeed possible to apply the Residual Income model to banks to provide a reasonable valuation.

When the value of a bank is estimated using the Residual Income model as defined in equation (16), the results show a high correlation between the market price and the estimated value, and thus the value explains a large percentage of cross-sectional variations in market prices. The goodness of fit of the results is around 80% at a confidence level of 99%. As a result, similar to companies in non-financial industries, it can be argued that the model provides a robust indication of the value of a bank, given its perceived risk as compared to the market portfolio.

Besides the institutions that make up the vast majority of the financial markets there are, however, other players in this field that have not been included in the research outlined in the previous sections such as credit unions, Islamic financial institutions, and micro finance institutions. Based on results from a small sample of Islamic Banks, it appears that the model should be able to provide a reasonably accurate value for all parts of the financial industry. Some further observations can be made as follows:

1. **Islamic Financial Institutions**

   Historically, Islamic and conventional finance have developed based on the same core principle, which is to provide financial intermediation between holders of surplus funds and those requiring funds for investment. Apart from the fact that Islamic finance operates based on the principles of the *Qur'an,* which prohibits both interest and speculation, the main difference between the Islamic and conventional banking industry is related to the further development of the industries. The first conventional banks started in the 17th century, but Islamic banks only started operating in their current form in 1963. Because the Islamic banking industry as we know it now is still relatively young, there are a number of issues related to availability and transparency of data. Moreover, Islamic banks operate mainly in countries where the capital market is not fully developed, so that share prices for such banks are either not set in an efficient market environment or are not available at all.

2. Micro Finance

Micro credit is the provision of loans to the unemployed, poor entrepreneurs and others living in poverty that are generally deemed to be unbankable. They typically lack collateral, steady employment and credit history and, therefore, do not have access to traditional means of credit. Traditional banks see these borrowers as high risk and don't want to extend credit. Micro credit is often extended to women to engage in self-employment projects that allow them to generate income. The loans are very small. To put it all in perspective, when Muhammad Yunus started Grameen Bank, he extended a total of $27 in loans which he lent to 42 people. In order to enhance the chance of repayment, micro credit institutions often use a system of "solidarity groups". They provide a support network for each other's efforts, as well as some social pressure. In combination with active management and extensive support for clients, around 90% of the loans are repaid on time and in full. Although a cost-intensive operation, it is also one of reduced credit risk. Further costs are incurred when it comes to regulatory capital requirements. Because the transactions are typically not backed by collateral, the risk profile is deemed to be higher resulting in additional capital requirements. There are additional costs due to the potentially high transaction volume, particularly low transaction size and operational costs per transaction that are at least the same compared with larger financial transactions. On the other hand, micro credit clients don't only take credit; they also save with the micro credit institution, thereby creating a co-operative or building society type institution.

3. **Socially Responsible Investing**

Socially Responsible or ethical investing is concerned with investing in sustainable and environmentally-friendly opportunities. It seeks to maximise financial return as well as the social good. Socially responsible investors generally favour corporations that promote environmental stewardship, consumer protection, human rights and diversity. Some investors avoid businesses involved in alcohol, gambling, weapons and other industries. The decision to include or exclude any investment lies with the individual investor. In itself, Socially Responsible Investing is not a new phenomenon. In 1690, John Fraeme and Thomas Gould started trading as Goldsmith Bankers in Lombard Street (London, United Kingdom) and subsequently incorporated the name Barclay in 1736 when the son-in-law of one of the founders became a partner in the business. Over time, this developed into Barclays Bank. In 1765, John Taylor and Sampson Lloyd started Lloyds bank in Birmingham (United Kingdom). Both Barclays and Lloyds are examples of banks whose business was strongly rooted in the puritan values that came with their Quaker heritage and which are largely similar to the principles underlying Socially Responsible Investing.

Neither of these institutions are non-profit. On the contrary, both are concerned with making a profit within the framework of their operations and associated principles. As such, it should be equally possible to apply a residual income model to determine the value of these financial institutions, as long as their specific business model is taken into consideration.

FURTHER OBSERVATIONS

4 Valuing in Uncertain Times

> *"Pursue a straightforward, upright, legitimate banking business. Never be tempted by the prospect of large returns to do anything but what may properly be done under the National Currency Act. Splendid financiering is not legitimate banking and splendid financiers are generally either humbugs or rascals."*
> *Hugh McCulloch, First Comptroller of the Currency, 1863*[22]

At the time of writing of this book it was no longer a certainty that big banks would be around forever and as many journalists and politicians kept on insisting the financial industry as we knew it had come to an end. Subprime mortgages and excessive risk taking has resulted in the bankruptcy of Lehman Brothers and the mass nationalisation of banks around the world. Everything we know about the financial industry including the regulatory environment has been questioned. Was it all the fault of the bankers? Probably not. Was all of it the regulator's fault then? Probably not either. Is it, as some would like us to believe, unique in the history of finance? Not even that.

Interestingly enough, as the "Grumpy Old Bankers"[23] point out, there is nothing new about this crisis, we have seen it all before. From the Tulip bubble in the 1600s via the South Sea bubble, the dot.com boom and the subprime crisis, asset inflation has been part of the financial industry just as much as Asset Backed Securities, Premium Bonds and Government Debt.

4.1 What Recent Data Tells Us

Hindsight is a wonderful thing, and many have seriously believed that there was indeed a new economic order. The question that arises is whether it would have been possible to predict, or at least foresee,

---

[22] Centre for the Study of Financial Innovation (CSFI), 2009 *Grumpy Old Bankers: Wisdom from Crisis Past.* London: CSFI, 10

[23] As above

events leading up to the credit crunch or the Great Depression by applying fundamental analysis. From the results presented in Chapter 2, it has become apparent that share price inflation in the run-up to a crisis reduces the goodness of fit of the Residual Income Model which measures how closely the estimated fundamental value matches the share price. In the run-up to an asset bubble, the spread between the share price and the estimated fundamental value widens, and as a result the goodness of fit reduces. During the period of the original study from 1993 until 2002, two crises occurred reasonably close after each other, the Asian crisis, closely followed by the dot.com boom. During the period 2003 – 2007 the global financial sector built itself up towards the biggest crisis since the Great Depression. In this section, a longer period of data is used to evaluate how price and estimated value have fared over time.

4.1.1 The Data

Between 2003 and 2008, eighty of the banks that were part of the original sample have either voluntarily or mandatorily merged with other institutions or have ceased to exist altogether. As a result, no data is available from Datastream on these entities. Mellon Financial for instance merged with Bank of New York in 2008 and although the key financial data can be obtained from their annual report filing (report 10K) with the Securities and Exchange Commission (SEC), the analyst consensus forecast data is no longer available. Similar to the construction of the original sample outlined in section 2.3, these entities have been removed from the total sample, resulting in a total sample of 114 banks for which sufficient data is available up to and including the end of December 2008. Added to this sample is ABN AMRO Bank for which, due to a takeover, data is available up to the end of December 2007, but no data is recorded for the year 2008. However, the impact of ABN AMRO's operations in 2008 is proportionally represented in the results of the banks that were part of the consortium that bought the bank. The total sample size used here is therefore 115.

4.1.2 The Statistics

Using panel data analysis, the test results for the original period spanning 1993 – 2002 showed that the fundamental value estimated using the Residual Income Model explains in excess of 80% of the price with a 99% probability. Extending this period to end in 2008, unsurprisingly results in a slightly lower explanatory value but, even given the tumultuous circumstances starting early 2007, over the period it can still be concluded that in excess of 78% of the share price is based on the estimated fundamental value.

Looking at the average price and estimated fundamental value for all 115 banks in the sample, over the period, it becomes clear how the observed deterioration in the goodness of fit between price and estimated fundamental value occurs.

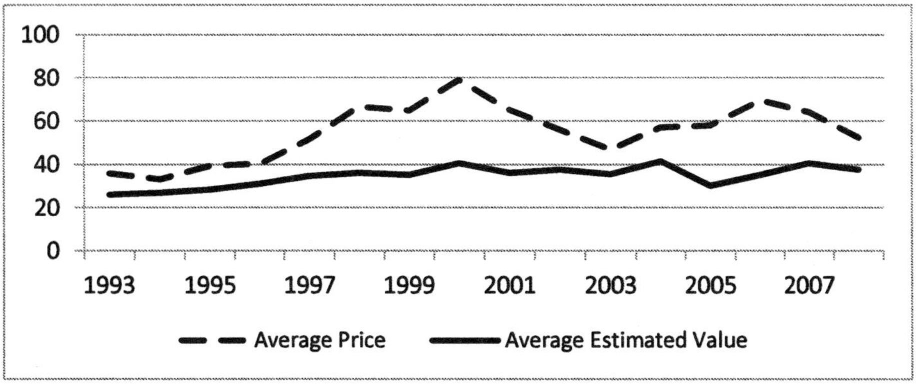

Figure 1 – Average price and average estimated fundamental value 1993 – 2008 (in $mn)

Figure 1 above, clearly shows a steep increase in prices from around 1996 to 1998, with the average estimated fundamental value remaining roughly at the same level. In the middle of 1997, the Asian crisis occurred which resulted in significant writing down of holdings in Asian currencies. The crisis, which had an impact on the global economy, did not result in a major drop of the average price of the banks in the sample. There can be a multitude of reasons for this, such as the implementation of effective hedging strategies or having relatively small holdings in the currencies affected. On the other hand, this was also the period of the dot.com bubble which started to slowly build up from 1995 onwards. This may explain why the Asian crisis did not result in a price decline, but instead resulted in prices stabilising over the next two years. Prices subsequently rose until during 2001 the dot.com bubble burst. From 2001 onwards, prices kept on declining until 2004, then increased again towards 2007 and declined again. Given the severity of the current financial crisis, the years 2001 – 2008 do not appear to accurately reflect the actual developments in the market.

One of the disadvantages of using average per share prices is that mergers, stock splits and the issue of additional shares result in a declining share price which is unrelated to market movements. In addition, average price per share data is distorted by banks that have a high share price and a low number of shares. In order to improve our view of the development of the global markets, the total estimated fundamental value and total price are used to provide a fuller picture of the developments.

In order to achieve this, both the price per share and the estimated fundamental value per share are multiplied by the number of shares and added up to provide a total for the sample of 115 banks.

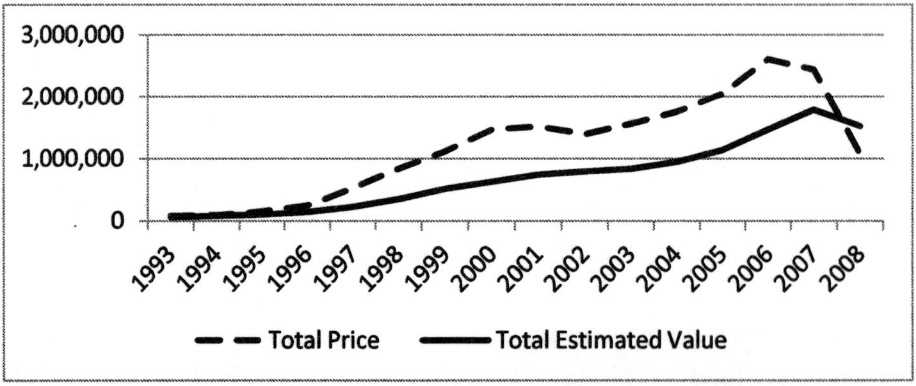

Figure 2 – Total price and total estimated fundamental value 1993 – 2008 (in $mn)

Figure 2 shows that the impact of the combined Asian crisis and dot.com bubble results in a relatively flat price movement from 2000 – 2001 with a slight reduction in 2002. The total estimated fundamental value does not appear to be impacted, and continues to increase gradually over the period, a development which continued through to 2007 when the price fell slightly followed by the rapid decline at the start of the current financial crisis.

Compared to previous years, 2008 is the first time the total price is below the total estimated fundamental value. This may be a consequence of the uncertainty surrounding the extent of the occurrences and the lack of information on how individual banks were affected by the sub-prime crisis. As a result of this, in combination with the additional capital and major write-downs announced, shareholders were actively selling in a market where demand had as good as disappeared. As can be observed from Figure 2, analysts have also reduced their forward expectations resulting in a lower total estimated value.

Not all banks in the sample are affected in the same way. During the sample period, and particularly during 2008, the number of American banks has reduced to a larger extent than the European banks. In part this is due to increased M&A activity over the period. In addition, many had recently been closed by their respective state's Department of Financial Institutions. This process typically involves appointing the Federal Deposit Insurance Corporation (FDIC) as a receiver whose first priority is to find a bank that takes on the responsibility for all deposits. As a result of these developments, however, the geographical distribution of the banks has changed as represented in Figure 3.

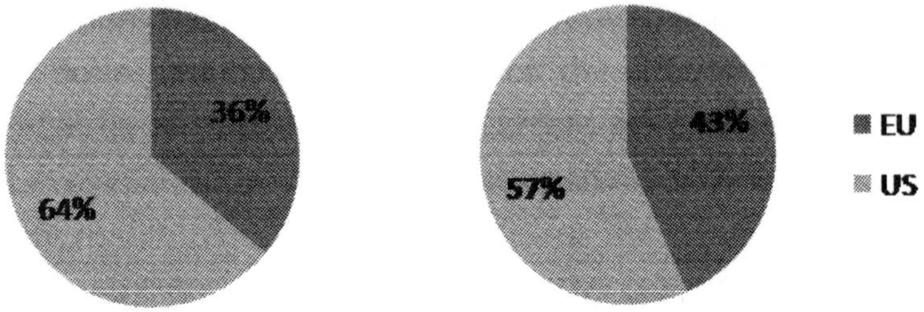

Figure 3 – Geographical distribution of the original (left) and final (right) sample

Looking at the two main geographical areas individually, it becomes clear that different areas have responded to the financial crisis in different ways.

The United States

Compared to the total sample as represented in Figure 2, the data for the United States represented in Figure 4 below, shows that the average total price for the 65 US banks in the sample is generally further away from the estimated fundamental value. In addition reactions to the various crises in the earlier periods appear to be more pronounced, such as the price reduction at the end of the dot.com boom.

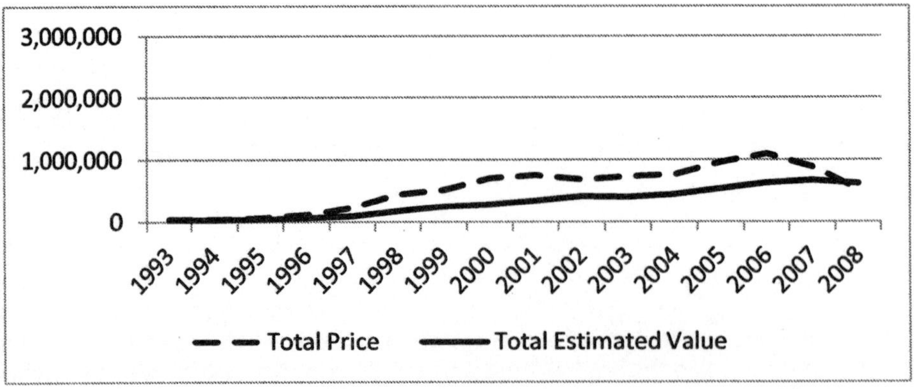

Figure 4 –Total price and total estimated fundamental value in the US 1993 – 2008 (in $mn)

In addition, prices seem to decline rapidly from 2006 onwards, without first showing signs of stabilisation, and do not drop as far below the estimated fundamental value as the overall banks in the sample.

The European Union

Banks in the European Union have seemingly suffered less from the dot.com boom as can be seen in the data of the remaining 50 European based banks represented in Figure 5. For the European banks, the price generally seems to move closer to the estimated fundamental value, but the drop in 2007 appears to be more severe than for the American banks. Towards the end of 2006, the potential write-offs associated with the subprime mortgage market are starting to become clear, but are at that point in time still thought to be largely restricted to the American market. As a result, the price of European banks still showed a marginal increase compared to 2005. As the full impact on European banks started to become clear, the prices began to fall significantly.

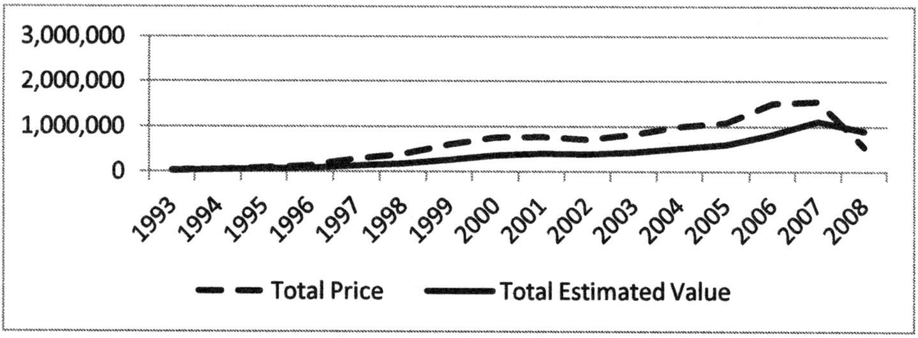

Figure 5 –Total price and total estimated fundamental value in the EU 1993 – 2008 (in $mn)

Equally, the estimated fundamental value has declined, but to a larger extent than the estimated fundamental value for the American banks in the sample.

Reasons for different behaviour of prices per region

There could be a number of reasons for the differences in the development of price and estimated fundamental value between the United States and Europe, and they are difficult to establish while the credit crisis is still developing. However, some of the reasons could include:

- *Market emotions*. Investors, faced with substantial uncertainty over the value of their investments, may have experienced panic and sold in large quantities disregarding fundamental values. Excess supply and a relative lack of demand resulted in significant price reductions.
- *Efficient Hedges*. Some of the banks in the sample may have implemented more efficient hedges than others. Some of the banks that received funds from the US Government under the Troubled Asset Relief Program (TARP) have openly admitted that their hedges on the demise of Lehman's and AIG generously off-set the losses incurred.
- *Size of Exposure*. Some of the banks in the sample will have had little or no exposure to any of the assets underlying the various asset bubbles.
- *Effectiveness of government measures*. Particularly in the current credit crisis, the effectiveness of the combined government measures including the nationalisation of banks and measures to motivate spending and investments will play an important role in the development of price and fundamental value.
- *Timing*. At the start of the current credit crisis, the expectation was that the problems with subprime mortgages were restricted to the United States and did not impact any other jurisdiction. As time passed, however, it became clear that the financial system is truly global and many other banks had also incurred large losses as a result of their exposure to derivative products based on these mortgages.

The after-effects of the crisis have, however, been severe and are showing in different ways. Banks previously considered too big to fail have been nationalised at the cost of significantly increased national debts. In addition, trust, one of the main cornerstones of the financial markets, had fallen out of the market and is, even in 2012, not yet restored. As a result, the financial markets are suffering and interbank lending is at a very low level which, for example, shows by the fact that deposits at the European Central Bank (ECB) are reported to be significantly higher than average.

The on-going uncertainty about whether or not the Greek government will repay its debt and, if so, to what extent it is putting additional pressure on the European financial industry. European based banks, many previously bailed out by their national governments, appear to have significant exposure to Greek government debt.

With the current high levels of national debt another bail-out of banks is unlikely, but only time will tell whether this will be required.

Part 2

Current Issues and Challenges

Part 2 of this book looks into a variety of issues associated with financial institutions which may have an impact on how they are perceived. Some of these will influence how banks are valued, others are more of a general nature. Did the Value at Risk measure work and if not, why not? What is the impact of news on stock prices, and how does behavioural finance come into play? These questions, as well as responses to financial crises, and a history of the prohibition of interest will be reviewed in this section.

5 The Challenge with Value at Risk

> *"The story that I have to tell is marked all the way through by a persistent tension between those who assert that the best decisions are based on quantification and numbers, determined by the patterns of the past, and those who base their decisions on more subjective degrees of belief about the uncertain future. This is a controversy that has never been resolved."*
> *Peter L. Bernstein – Against the Gods*[24]

As outlined in section 2.2.4, banks are subject to a variety of risks, which are typically measured in aggregate using Value at Risk (VaR). Although initially devised as a measure to report financial risks, it was soon used to attempt to measure the downside risk of either a portfolio or, in aggregation, a firm into one single number. It is very much a numbers-based methodology based on past patterns. The output of a VaR equation attempts to measure the downside risk taking into account financial leverage and diversification effects across all markets and instruments. It represents the maximum amount a bank is likely to stand to lose on a given day or over a number of days (e.g. over a period of one week), generally with a confidence interval of 95% or 99%.

There are three main types of VaR, each with their own strengths and weaknesses:

- **Historical VaR**. The Historical VaR estimates the nth percentile in potential losses based on historical returns on the relevant traded assets. Historical VaR measures potential portfolio risk one to two years ahead using the previous years (typically anywhere between one and twenty, but more often than not spanning one to two years) as a benchmark.

---

[24] Bernstein, Peter L. (1998) *Against the Gods: The Remarkable Story of Risk* New York: John Wiley & Sons

- **Variance-Covariance VaR**. The Variance-Covariance VaR takes the historical volatility and correlation of returns on traded assets into consideration when calculating the nth percentile in potential losses. Variance-Covariance VaR is again typically based on historic data covering a period of two to ten years.
- **Monte Carlo VaR**. Monte Carlo is a commonly used simulation technique which is used to simulate a variety of different scenarios for the portfolio value on the target date. The Monte Carlo VaR method approximates the behaviour of financial prices using simulations to generate random price paths. The result is a forward-looking simulation of the environment, rather than one focusing on the historical data used for Historical and Variance-Covariance VaR.

Over time, banks started to use VaR as a risk control tool. Trading limits were complemented by VaR limits, and at a firm level it was used to control firm-wide risk-taking diversification into account. From an initially passive tool, it started to develop into a tool to control risk and subsequently into a risk allocation tool. It is designed to incorporate traditional risks and risks related to adverse market movements of financial derivatives and structured products. In addition, VaR is often used as a basis to calculate the amount of economic capital required to support a business, which is an essential component of economic value added measures.

5.1 The Beauty of VaR

No matter which VaR framework is used, the result of the equation provides a single amount that is deemed to be the maximum value a bank is exposed to over the coming period – generally one week or ten days – with a very high level of confidence. For example, a one-week VaR of $100 million with a 99% confidence level indicates that there is a 99% chance that the portfolio will not lose more than $100 million over the next week.

Another advantage of VaR is that is can measure risks at different levels very quickly. It can be applied to individual contracts, portfolios, a trader's position but also firm-wide, and can generally be made available within a short time.

Because of these advantages, banks used the VaR to meet the Securities and Exchange Committee (SEC) requirements for quantitative disclosure of market risk in the financial statement. The Basel Committee on Banking Supervision went even further and allowed banks to rely on their own internal VaR calculations to define capital requirements to support market risk.

5.2 How VaR has Fared

Although implemented widely, VaR has not necessarily fared very well during the current crisis for a number of reasons. Generally, most implementations of VaR assume that the portfolio of assets and liabilities that are part of the analysis stays constant over the one-period or 10-day horizon. On 28th January 2008, Bloomberg.com[25] reported that at a time that Merrill Lynch's reported losses on CDOs had already reached $18 billion, their historical VaR was reported to be $92 million. How does this occur, and what is the issue with VaR?

First of all, VaR mainly provides an indication of the maximum risk a bank is exposed to under the assumption that the distribution of the underlying price data is approximately normal, which, as we know, is not necessarily the case. In addition, the question of what happens outside the confidence interval (e.g. the other 1%) is not really addressed. But that is exactly where the current issues partly come from, the incidents commonly referred to as "Black Swans"[26]. A Black

---

[25] Death of VAR Evoked as Risk Taking Vim Meets Taleb's Black Swan

[26] The theory was described by Nassim Nicholas Taleb in his 2007 book *The Black Swan*. The term *Black Swan* comes from the assumption that 'All swans are white'. In that context, a *black swan* was a symbol for something that could not exist. The 18th Century discovery of black swans in Western Australia was first used by John Stuart Mill to illustrate that a perceived impossibility can be contradicted by a new discovery.

Swan is defined as an incident that is incredibly rare and is therefore not considered a possibility. Take for example the collapse of Long Term Capital Management (LTCM) which was due to the fact that under normal market circumstances the Asian and the Russian crisis could not have occurred simultaneously. When the market did not return to what was considered to be "normal" but LTCM was still trading as if it would, they eventually went bust.

There are other challenges associated with the VaR methodology. VaR relies heavily on historical data which does not necessarily repeat itself. In addition, the historical data generally only covers a relatively short period, which in turn implies that extreme circumstances are not necessary taken into consideration.

Box 8 – The Use of Historic Data, an Example

A significant proportion of the implementations of VaR apply a two-year historic data period to determine the Value at Risk. The VaR on a subprime mortgage portfolio would have been much lower than the real exposure to risk incurred because during the period 2006 – 2007 house prices did not decrease. If a longer period of historic data had been used which would have included the previous house price crash of 1989, the VaR on the same portfolio is likely to have been significantly higher. Although, even then, the accuracy of the resulting VaR number may not have been correct.

The impact of adverse movements in available liquidity is not included in the assumptions underlying the model, which is another reason why VaR underperforms in the current crisis. The significant reduction in liquidity and the associated widening of credit spreads is not something that is typically included in the analysis as a likely scenario. The London Interbank Offer Rate (LIBOR) has always been assumed to have a small spread over government paper and futures, an assumption that was disproved during the late 2008 and 2009 credit crunch when the LIBOR rates quoted were well in excess of the central banks' base rates. On top of that, the rates actually charged by banks in the capital markets were significantly higher than the LIBOR rates quoted. Institutions relying heavily on the capital markets for their funding such as Northern Rock and HBOS in the United Kingdom were either forced into nationalisation or being taken over. Their business models, which relied on arbitrage between the interest on retail mortgages and the cost of funds in the capital markets, failed as a result of the inverted yield curves.

Banks are particularly susceptible to systematic risk, which is the risk posed to the financial system or the (global) economy. The failure of a major financial institution can result in a domino effect throughout the financial industry which has the potential to bring down an economy. Not only will their depositors lose any money which is not covered by a guarantee scheme, they are also likely to renege on their obligations as counterparties towards other financial institutions. This, in turn, will result in financial pressures on these individuals and institutions who may subsequently have to renege on some of their obligations and so on and so forth. Given a global financial infrastructure, this can potentially have far reaching consequences.

Box 9 – The Far Reaching Impact of Non-Settlement

In June 1974, a small, relatively unknown bank in Germany, Bank Herstatt, had its banking licence withdrawn and was ordered into liquidation effective from the close of the German interbank payments system at 3:30 in the afternoon on the 26th of June 1974. During the morning before Herstatt's banking licence was withdrawn, some of their counterparties had made irrevocable payments in Deutsche Mark to satisfy their payment obligations in foreign exchange transactions against US Dollars. These payments were made in good faith in the anticipation of the receipt of the US Dollar equivalent later that day. When Herstatt's licence was withdrawn at 3:30 in the afternoon German time, it was only 10:30 in the morning in New York. The correspondent bank suspended all outgoing US Dollar payments with immediate effect, leaving Herstatt's counterparties fully exposed to the value of the Deutsche Mark paid earlier that day, without any receipt of the corresponding amounts in US Dollar. Subsequently, some of the counterparties could not directly fulfil the US Dollar obligations they had to other parties resulting in a domino effect.

VaR does not really incorporate the effects of a global, highly correlated financial market. On the contrary, VaR typically assumes that assets are liquid and can easily be sold at, or at least near, the current market value. In the event that a financial institution has to liquidate assets urgently to realise capital, the law of supply and demand dictates that the price will be negatively impacted, which is a result of higher supply at a consistent or lower level of demand. This has a further negative effect on the bank being able to meet its obligations.

Looking at the current crisis, another challenge associated with VaR is that many of the losses in the current crisis have occurred on assets that are non-traded such as subprime mortgage loans, Alt-A mortgages[27] and structured products that use the former as reference

[27] Alt-A stands for Alternative A-paper. Alt-A mortgages are a type of US mortgage which are riskier than prime mortgages due to conditions such as a lower credit

collateral. Because they are non-traded, they are often not included in the VaR calculations, with all the associated consequences. Subprime and Alt-A mortgages packaged up in Mortgage Backed Securities (MBS) were generally assigned a high credit rating, in part justified by the diversification effect. However, under the US mortgage regime, a lender can easily put the house back to the bank when the value of the house declines. Subprime mortgages, typically, have low deposits and the chance of default is generally higher than with other mortgages.

The VaR calculation also assumes that the portfolio will remain unchanged. No assets will mature, and no assets will either be bought or sold. Although this may be a workable assumption for a very short time period, in a market where trades take place on a near continuous basis, it is highly unlikely. And if all that was not enough, the Monte Carlo VaR assumes that the returns in a period are independent from the previous period, which is a flawed concept. The majority of returns are highly cyclical and will be dependent on previous period returns, particularly when considering potential defaults or price movements. Finally, VaR involves estimations of future values, correlation and other factors each of which can result in estimation errors.

Overall, it would be safe to say that VaR has many disadvantages. These appear to be mainly associated with events that, to say the least, can be considered to be unusual. But still, the high confidence level appears to have resulted in a false sense of security.

5.3 Is VaR all bad?

Boldly saying that VaR is all bad and should never be used again is probably a classic case of throwing the baby out with the bathwater. There is a lot to say against VaR. The use of short-term historic data, the black swans, the fact that non-traded instruments are not included are

---

score, a higher loan-to-value or because they are extended on investment properties.

all issues that may need to be addressed. However, it does provide a single number that is easy to understand. Although it may be flawed, it is still the best number out there when it comes to a firm's risk. The next question will then have to be "where to from here?"

First, the VaR methodology could be enhanced significantly if issues such as recognition of cyclicality and defaults and the inclusion of non-traded assets are addressed. On the other hand, this may potentially be an expensive exercise and could lead to other challenges. In addition, the VaR number should probably be given a lot less individual importance. Rather than looking at the output on a day-to-day basis, the trend is where changes in risk will be spotted, and that can then be analysed further. VaR is not an all-knowing methodology; it would have to be used as a tool in combination with other risk management tools such as, for instance, Risk Adjusted Return on Capital (RAROC), the purpose of which is to adjust trading profits by the remuneration of risk capital. RAROC recognises that trading positions with a higher risk profile require a larger amount of economic capital to absorb larger potential losses. If we remember that VaR does not look at what could happen in the other 1% of the time, and keep the liquidity of the instruments as well as the markets in mind it can still play a significant role in the overall risk assessment process.

In any case, any risk taken by a bank will have to be evaluated against its risk management system, as well as the cost of the measures in place. The complexity of banks seriously hinders simple assessment of the risks taken and how they are controlled. It will never be possible to incorporate safeguards against all risks within the risk management system of a bank. A more complex risk management system may actually make the situation worse, due to the increasing complexity that is introduced, as well as potentially creating a false sense of security.

6 The Impact of News and Behavioural Finance

Valuation models generally assume that investors exhibit rational behaviour when they make their investment decisions. The severe reductions in stock prices that occurred during the second half of 2008 and early 2009, however, support the theory that investors may react to news in a way that is not purely based on fundamental values. This chapter explores the Efficient Market Hypothesis, behavioural finance and the response of investors to news.

6.1 Efficient Market Hypothesis

The efficient market hypothesis is based on the notion that all available information is directly incorporated in the price of a security, and arbitrage based on information is therefore impossible. Nearly all valuation and asset pricing theories assume that the market behaves in this way. Over time, research has shown that not all markets are equally efficient, and three forms of the efficient market hypothesis can be distinguished[28]:

Weak-form efficient market

In a weak-form efficient market, it is not possible for an investor to earn excess returns by developing trading rules based on historical price or return information. In these markets, any information available beyond historical prices and returns is not necessarily reflected in the share price. Whether this information is publicly available or not is irrelevant, and trading typically takes place on the basis of information available to the individual investor which could include insider information. In these markets, investors can enhance their returns by implementing a trading strategy of seeking out over- or undervalued stocks.

---

[28] Copeland, T.E and J.F. Weston (1992) *Financial Theory and Corporate Policy* Third Edition, New York: Addison Wesley Publishing Company

Semi-strong form efficient market

In a semi-strong form efficient market, all publicly available information is immediately and fully reflected in the share price. Trading strategies seeking out over- or undervalued stocks will only result in a potential profit for the investor if he has insider information available to him.

Strong-form efficient market

In a strong-form efficient market, all publicly available information is immediately and fully reflected in the share price and insider trading is prohibited. The prohibition of insider trading is generally implemented within a legal and/or regulatory framework. Investors cannot earn any excess returns purely based on company information available to them.

Results of event studies have indicated that stock prices generally tend to adjust quickly to information about investment decisions, dividend changes, changes in capital structure, and corporate control transactions. All of these findings support the semi-strong form of the efficient market hypothesis concluding that any publicly available information will be incorporated in the share price almost instantaneously. However, the majority of these studies have been executed in American and European markets, where value-relevant private information appears to be rare, and where markets are classified as semi-strong form efficient.

In emerging markets, however, prices do not necessarily reflect all available information. Trading is often restricted to a few hours per day. Kuwait Stock Exchange's trading hours, for example, are 9:15 – 12:15 for the Spot Market and 12:45 – 13:15 for the Futures Market, and Bahrain Stock Exchange's trading hours are 10:00 – 13:00. Not all stocks are traded on a daily basis and both volume and value of trades are typically quite low. In addition, purchase and sale decisions are often driven by personal motives such as how well someone gets on with the chairman of a company and not necessarily on private or public information. The characteristics of these markets result in the fact that they cannot be classified as efficient, potentially not even in its weakest form. Fama[29] has done extensive research into the effectiveness of markets and found as early as 1970 that "The current price of a security 'fully reflects' all available information", and thus that there is such a thing as an efficient market. This forms the basis for the Random Walk Theory of weak-form efficiency.[30] Only when extensive testing appeared to support the efficiency hypothesis at this level, did research move on to semi-strong and strong-form tests.

6.2 Behavioural Finance

The conventional banks that are part of the underlying study are all based in semi-strong form efficient markets where prices are deemed to incorporate all available information quickly. However, the severe price changes in the current market circumstances further confirm the findings in behavioural finance that the agents in the market are not necessarily rational. After all, as early as 1912, Selden[31] wrote *Psychology of the Stock Market* "upon the belief that the movements of prices on the exchanges are dependent to a very considerable degree on the mental attitude of the investing and trading public".

In 1957, Simon[32] introduced the concept of bounded rationality which recognises that people do not base all their decisions on fact but are influenced by other elements. The human mind has limitations and does not have the capacity to understand everything, particularly when complexity increases. In addition, there is only limited time available in which to reach decisions and people are generally influenced by the

---

[29] Fama, E.F. (1970) *Efficient Capital Markets: A Review of Theory and Empirical Work*, The Journal of Finance, 25(2), 383-417

[30] The Random Walk Theory states that the entire distribution is independent of the information available. Initial studies on efficient markets were further concerned with weak-form efficient markets in which the information subset of interest is just past price (or return) histories.

[31] Selden, G. C., (1912) *Psychology of the Stock Market: Human Impulses Lead To Speculative Disasters*. New York: Ticker Publishing

[32] Simon, Herbert (1957) *Models of Man, Social and Rational: Mathematical Essays on Rational Human Behavior in a Social Setting*. New York: Wiley

perceived quality of a news source. As a result, Simon argues that decisions are not fully thought through and people can only be rational within limits.

Research by Boston College, Massachusetts[33] shows that public news releases can have a significant impact on the price of different types of U.S. Treasury bonds. Out of a number of news issues available such as Nonfarm payroll, and the change in unemployment level, consumer price index and the Treasury budget, only those are selected that are deemed to be surprising, i.e. where the news is either better or worse than generally expected by the market. Although the effects of these surprise announcements vary according to maturity, public news can explain a substantial portion of price volatility during the period almost immediately following the announcement. This particular research finds that prices move significantly before any increase in volume is observed, which creates the suggestion that the initial price adjustment is mainly driven by public information. Trading volume and price volatility increases have been observed to persist for around 60 minutes, but the bid-ask spreads reverted back to normal about 15 minutes after the announcement. This in itself suggests that a second phase of price adjustments exists during which both volatility and volume are partly driven by informed trading. Even beyond the 15 minute period trading persists at an above average level. These findings support earlier research, which find similar reactions to news for other asset classes such as futures[34].

A more recent study by Roache and Rossi[35] shows that unexpected

---

[33] Balduzzi, P., J.E. Elton and T.C. Green (2001) *Economic News and Bond Prices: Evidence from the U.S. treasury Market*, Journal of Financial and Quantitative Analysis, Vol 36, No 4, 523 – 543 Seattle: University of Washington School of Business Administration

[34] Ederington, L. H., and J. H. Lee (1993) *How Markets Process Information: News Releases and Volatility* Journal of Finance, Vol 48, 1161-1191

[35] Roache, Shaun K. and M. Rossi (2009) *The Effects of Economic News on Commodity Prices: Is Gold Just Another Commodity?* IMF Working paper 09/140, Washington: IMF

announcement of economic indicators has an almost direct impact on the prices of various commodities, although the exact impact varies according to the type of commodity. One of their main findings is that gold prices react to specific scheduled announcements in the United States and the Euro area (e.g. indicators of activity such as the employment data and payroll or interest rate decisions). They find that the way in which the gold price reacts is consistent with its traditional role as a safe-haven and store of value, which is contrary to the response of other commodity prices to significant news items.

Previous literature on the impact of macroeconomic announcements has focussed mainly on bond and currency markets, but there is fairly clear and consistent evidence that macroeconomic news has significant price and volatility effects. In some cases the reaction happens on the same day, but in other cases the impact is not visible until the next day. Although a large range of macroeconomic data is made publicly available, the impact on prices appears particularly significant in periods when uncertainty is high and when the news is related to the labour market, inflation and durable goods orders. Most academic research in this area is reviewing the impact of macroeconomic announcements on bond and currency markets, but it is reasonable to consider the impact that news generally may have on other commodities and equity prices.

It is not just macroeconomic news the market responds to. In 1996 Allan Greenspan, then chairman of the Federal Reserve Board coined the term *irrational exuberance* to describe the behaviour of stock market investors[36] in a televised speech in Washington. As soon as these words were mentioned stock markets dropped (DAX -4%, the Dow Jones -2.3%, FTSE -4%, Hang Seng -2.9% and Nikkei Index -3.2%) without any apparent reason. Robert Schiller[37] has since researched this

---

[36] Greenspan, A. (1996) *The Challenge of Central Banking in a Democratic Society*, speech before the American Enterprise Institute for Public Policy, Washington, 5th December 1996

[37] Schiller, R.J. (2005) *Irrational Exuberance* second edition, Princeton, New Jersey: Princeton University Press

issue further and concludes that the term itself has become useful to characterise the social phenomenon that occurs when markets have been bid up to unusually high and unsustainable levels under the influence of a naïve and optimistic market psychology. The sharp drop in share prices globally in late 2008/early 2009 was, at least in part, a case of correcting for earlier *"irrational exuberance"*. Considerable numbers of stocks were overvalued and a market correction was at that point long overdue. The significant price drop cannot, however, be explained entirely by a market correction. The initial news surrounding Lehman's bankruptcy caused investors to sell banking shares at heavily discounted prices. It soon became apparent that financial institutions that had previously announced positive profit expectations might actually have sustained significant losses. Due to a lack of transparency, increasing complexity of the financial instruments underpinning the crisis and the fact that no one appeared to know who was exposed to the credit risk on securitised financial assets, the extent of the losses that were sustained did not become clear until much later, adding even more uncertainty. Banks were nationalised or forced to take over other entities again which caused yet another layer of uncertainty. Investors responded to all the uncertainty perhaps excessively or even irrationally, but this is not necessarily unexpected and is in part associated with herd behaviour and reliance on certain news sources. Herd behaviour is however not necessarily irrational, especially when the investor is trading on someone else's behalf. Consider for instance a situation in which a trader decides to buy bank shares at a time when everyone else is selling. If he gets it right, he's a hero, but getting it wrong can have severe consequences for the trader. Whereas, if buying bank shares is regarded as an acceptable strategy followed by many and it goes wrong the individual typically does not get "punished" for his decision.

Box 10 - How media may influence investors

An interesting example of the influence of media on share prices is the Mad Money programme on CNBC. Various pieces of research have found[38] that the stock recommendations provided on the programme generally do not appear to outperform the market. Although no one can beat the market consistently, the buy and sell recommendations given on the Mad Money programme appear to lead to a consistent underperformance. Statistics show, however, that investors seem to act on the recommendations provided in the programme. It is unclear whether this is because they trust Cramer's decisions or whether investors take some form of comfort from the fact that the programme is broadcast by CNBC. In any case, it does show that not all investment decisions are rational. If investors acted rationally, they would undertake their own fundamental analysis as well and make an informed decision on whether to invest or not and not just act on the word of one man.

6.3 Is the Market Efficient?

Ultimately, investors do not base their investment decisions solely on fundamental analysis and available information. They rely on heuristics[39], the perceived credibility of the news source and other emotional and factors associated with perception[40]. Among the findings of a variety of research are the following:

- Long-term earnings forecasts made by security analysts tend to be biased toward recent successes;

---

[38] Alpert, B (2009) *Cramer's Star Outshines his Stock Picks* and *The Cramer Effect – and Defect* (February 2007), both of which also mention additional research. The articles were published on www.smartmoney.com/investing.

[39] The process by which people find out things for themselves, usually by trial and error.

[40] For further reading see for example Shefrin, H (2002) *Beyond Greed and Fear: Understanding Behavioral Finance and the Psychology of Investing.* Oxford: Oxford University Press

- Analysts tend to be more optimistic about recent winners than recent losers;
- Investors have different attitudes to risk, which influences the individual's decision process.
- When making decisions under uncertainty, people tend to apply what is known as the *Minimax Regret Criterion.* Given a choice most people are biased towards avoiding a certain loss, but will take a chance on a smaller loss since the probability of loss reduction has a strong attraction to the decision maker. Under uncertainty, the decision maker measures the opportunity cost (regret) associated with each possible course of action and selects the action that minimises the maximum regret. Regret is in this case measured as the difference between the best and the worst outcome for each course of action.

There are more examples of how emotions and perceptions influence investor decisions and hence share prices. Behavioural finance certainly plays a role when it comes to share prices.

However, despite all of the evidence to the contrary discussed above, the efficient market theory still plays a significantly larger part in the valuation of firms. Generally, research into the area has established that 80% of a company's share price is determined based on the fundamental value estimated of the firm which is estimated using, for instance, a Residual Income Model. This leaves only 20% or less open to investment decisions on elements other than fundamental value. In addition, the impact of behavioural finance is typically only noticed during a brief period. Share prices generally appear to be reverting back to the value based on their fundamental value after a relatively short period of time. All in all, although behavioural finance has some influence on share price movements, the bulk of the price is still made up of the estimated (future) value of a firm, particularly over the longer term.

7 Asset Bubbles, Regulations, and Politics

"Pursue a straightforward, upright, legitimate banking business. Never be tempted by the prospect of large returns to do anything but what may properly be done under the National Currency Act. Splendid financiering is not legitimate banking and splendid financiers are generally either humbugs or rascals."
Hugh McCulloch (1863) in a Circular Letter to the banks[41]

Financial crises generally follow a period of inflated asset prices also known as an asset bubble. The underlying asset typically exhibits an unjustifiably sharp increase in price mainly caused by a combination of excess demand and investor sentiment. During the build up of the asset bubble there is a collective belief in the sustainability of the value of the asset. The first recorded bubble, Tulip Mania, occurred in 1624 – 1637. During the period November 1636 to February 1637, prices of tulip bulbs multiplied twentyfold. In early February 1637 rumours that trade was to be suspended took hold and prospective buyers no longer bid for the tulips for sale. By the 1st of May 1637, price levels were roughly at the level they were on the 12th of November 1636[42].

Unlike later asset bubbles, the bursting of the Tulip bubble did not result in a financial crisis. Not only was the hype restricted to a relatively small number of players[43], but retrospective amendments were made to contracts written between November 1636 and May 1637 converting the original futures contracts to option type contracts giving the florists the right, but not the obligation, to buy the bulbs at

---

[41] McCulloch, H (1863) *Circular Letter of the Treasury Department, Office of the Comptroller of the Currency.* As quoted in Centre for the Study of Financial Innovation (CSFI), 2009 *Grumpy Old Bankers: Wisdom from Crisis Past.* London: CSFI, p 10

[42] Thompson, E.A. (2007), *The tulipmania: Fact or artifact?* Public Choice 130(1–2): 99–114

[43] Dash, M (1999) *Tulipomania* London: Victor Gollancz

the prevailing market price on the exercise date[44].

The impact of later asset bubbles was less contained and exhibited contagious effects caused by interlinked financial markets. The aftermath of financial crises is no longer restricted to small groups or a single economy, but instead has a regional or even global impact. Similar to Tulip Mania, each of the asset bubbles that followed was intensified by a combination of expanding credit, greed, and a strong belief that this time it was all going to be different[45]. Unfortunately, there are no signs that we have collectively learned our lesson from any of the asset bubbles that have occurred to date, nor is it likely that we will. This chapter further explores the underlying causes of asset bubbles and the subsequent crisis, and the responses from politicians, regulators and the general public by comparing two of the major financial crises in modern history, the 1929 Stock Market Crash and the Credit Crunch of 2008.

7.1 Asset Bubbles and Financial Crises

Tulip Mania in the 1630s is the first recorded financial bubble, and was followed by, among others, the South Sea and the Mississippi bubbles in the 1720s, the Stock Market Crash in the 1920s, the real estate bubbles in Japan and Scandinavia in the 1980s, the Internet Hype and, most recently, the Credit Crunch. In all fairness, the latter is also not expected to be the last. Bubbles generally follow a non-sustainable pattern of price changes or cash flows fuelled by an expansion of money and credit, and eventually implode[46]. Neither the 1929 Stock Market crash nor the 2008 Credit Crunch – each of which will be reviewed in more detail in the remainder of this section – is an exception to this.

---

[44] Thompson (2007)

[45] Schoon, N (2009) *Valuing Banks in Uncertain Times* London: Spiramus Press

[46] Kindleberger, C.P. and R.Z. Aliber (2005) *Manias, Panics and Crisis – A History of Financial Crises* New York: Palgrave Macmillan p.1

7.1.1 The Stock Market Crash – 1929

The Great Depression, so named because *"Panic"* was deemed inappropriate by the Hoover administration[47], was triggered by the 1929 US Stock Market Crash. A long and deep decline of the American economy ensued starting in October 1929, which only started to show signs of recovery in March 1933.

A period of strong economic growth stimulated by the Second Industrial Revolution and the end of the American Civil War combined with the expansion of credit in the call-money[48] market in New York[49] resulted in highly inflated equity prices creating an asset bubble. In the period leading up to the Stock Market Crash, the amount of call-money outstanding in the US markets increased significantly from $6.4bn in December 1928 to $8.5bn in October 1929. The market crash that followed shows similarities with the collapse of the French banks and the subsequent crisis in 1873 – 1896, heavy speculation was combined with a decline in economic activity immediately prior to the stock market reaching its peak. When the stock market crashed, banks demanded repayment of outstanding loans to investors and brokers out of fear that, similar to 1873, the Stock Exchange might temporarily be closed which would have a severe impact on the banks' liquidity. This in turn caused problems for investors who made extensive use of margin credits, allowing them to finance securities transactions for 90% with borrowed money against a 10% down payment. As their credit was withdrawn, they were left with little choice but to default on transactions or margin calls[50]. Unsurprisingly, one of the regulations issued by the Federal Reserve Board relatively shortly after the Stock

---

[47] Brendon, P (2009) *With Bubbles, it's plus ça change...* Financial World, July/August 2009, London: CSFI

[48] Call-money generally refers to funds that are repayable on demand at any time, and are also known as callable or demand loans. By their nature, these funds provide short-term liquidity.

[49] Kindleberger and Aliber (2005), p 55

[50] Kindleberger and Aliber (2005) p 69-74

Market Crash was to curb the margin buying of stocks by setting the minimum margin requirements to 50%[51].

Increasing dividends and positive financial news up to October 1929 support the fact that initially the fundamental values of the companies were still deemed to be fine[52]. There were, however, also signals to the contrary. The Industrial Production Index and automobile production, both strong indicators of the American economy, exhibited a sharp decline[53] which cannot solely be explained by a shift in autonomous spending or a change in the money supply. Instead they are largely clarified by instability in the credit system which, at the time, was moving funds away from production and consumption into the call-money market[54]. Banks became increasingly cautious in their lending, thus creating a vicious circle of increasing instability of the supply of credit which eventually brought the markets down. Once the market crashed all credit was frozen, and a sharp decline in loans followed, clearly exposing both the instability of the credit system and the fragility of the financial infrastructure. A general decline in prices combined with a sharp reduction in available liquidity caused borrowers to default on their loans, further exacerbating the effects on the economy[55].

The markets only started to show signs of recovery after Roosevelt declared a bank holiday on the 6th of March 1933 effectively taking control of the problem of illiquid and insolvent financial institutions,

---

[51] This regulation, known as Regulation T, is still in force. www.sec.gov/investor/pubs/margin.htm

[52] Bierman, H (2010) *The 1929 Stock Market Crash* http://eh.net/encyclopedia/article/bierman.crash

[53] The Industrial Production Index fell from 127 in June 1929 to 99 in December 1929 and automobile production dropped from 440,000 in August 1929 to 92,500 in December.

[54] Kindleberger and Aliber (2005) p 69-74.

[55] Kindleberger and Aliber (2005) p 69-74

making its resolution an issue of the Federal Government[56].

Due to the high correlation of global stock markets the impact of the crash was not limited to the United States but spread to Europe and Asia. However, the faster the stock market prices fell, the higher the correlation between markets leading to an even further accumulation of losses, not sparing prudent investors who had applied geographic diversification to their portfolio to reduce their risk[57].

7.1.2 The Credit Crunch – 2008

Many asset bubbles have occurred since 1929, but none with the same global reach as the 2008 Credit Crunch and despite increasingly sophisticated risk management many people still admitted they had not seen it coming.

The generally accepted starting point of the Credit Crunch is the bursting of the subprime mortgage bubble. Subprime mortgages refer to mortgages in which the borrower has a lower than usual credit score combined with a higher than usual loan-to-value. These mortgages were mainly issued in the US as a result of policies and regulations specifically designed to increase home ownership and affordable housing across the population. Subsequently they were packaged and repackaged into Mortgage Backed Securities (MBS) which were sold to banks and institutional investors, resulting in investors globally having a significant exposure to the US housing market. Under normal circumstances subprime MBS would be classified as higher risk and would hence demand a higher return. Due to ever increasing real estate prices and the introduction of revenue protection using Credit Default Swaps (CDS) and Credit Default Obligations (CDO) the risks were, however, categorised as low. In the event of default by the borrower, the bank was expected to be able to recover its funds easily from the proceeds of the sale and the pay-out from CDSs and CDOs. The general

---

[56] Minsky, H.P. (1993) *Finance and Stability: The Limits of Capitalism* The Levy Economics Institute of Bard College, Working Paper number 93

[57] Kindleberger and Aliber (2005) p 108

precept on which the associated mortgage backed paper was sold as low-risk/high-return was twofold. On the one hand, the return was aggregated for the portfolio justifying the high return whilst on the other hand the risk was significantly reduced due to diversification benefits. The paper was typically rated as AAA[58] by the rating agencies and mainly sold to institutional investors and financial institutions.

A small number of market participants started to raise concerns over slack lending practices and excessive liquidity in the market in 2006 but it was not until 2007 that investors started to question the stability of the paper and banks became more and more cautious in their lending strategies[59]. Initially the reduction of available credit was confined to the US banks but, as a result of the interlinking of global financial markets, it soon spread to other jurisdictions.

Similar to the Stock Market Crash in 1929, instability of credit eventually caused the bubble to burst. Northern Rock in the UK is a case in point. Although it had exposure to higher risk mortgages, it was generally seen as running a solid and healthy mortgage book, with acceptable levels of defaults. However, unlike most banks, Northern Rock relied more on the short-term money market for their funding and less on depositors, which is evidenced by the fact that the proportion of borrowing covered by deposits fell from 62.3% of total liability in 1997 to an estimated 22.2% in 2006[60]. On the 9th of August 2007, the interbank and other financial markets froze, causing almost immediate concern for Northern Rock. This led to the run on the bank in September 2007 and its subsequent nationalisation[61] which was not caused by the quality of their mortgages but the lack of liquidity in the

---

[58] AAA is the highest available credit quality, signifying a very low probability of default.

[59] www.moneyweek.com/news-and-charts/the-wall-street-investor-who-shorted-subprime--and-made-15bn

[60] Milne, A. and G. Wood (2008), *Banking Crisis Solutions: Old and New* Review (Federal Reserve Bank of St Louis), September/October 2008, pp. 517–530.

[61] Milne and Wood (2008)

markets it strongly relied on[62].

By this time it started to become clear that, contrary to earlier belief, the crisis was not just contained to the US but was rapidly starting to have a global impact. In early March 2008, rumours started that perhaps Bear Stearns would not be able to meet its obligations, ultimately resulting in a rapid withdrawal of credit to the firm, culminating in the bank having to apply for emergency funding from the Federal Reserve on the 14th of March. Although this could not save the firm, it did tide them over until the orchestrated sale to JP Morgan for $10 per share which, although only a fraction of its 52-week high of $133.20, was still above the original offer of $2.00 per share[63]. In September of the same year Lehman Brothers, one of the banks deemed to be "too big to fail", was allowed to file for Chapter 11 bankruptcy protection. Global panic ensued with banks having to post significant losses and having to admit they were not sure what the final loss estimates would be.

Share prices dropped significantly and many banks had to be bailed out by their respective governments. Unfortunately they had to find out the hard way that a combination of low risk and high return does not exist.

7.1.3 Common underlying causes

In comparison with the Stock Market Crash in 1929, additional complexity was introduced in the 2008 Credit Crunch with the practice of splitting and repackaging mortgages into different tranches as a result of which investors often carried more risk than they were aware of. Even so, the common basis of both crises can be found in some remarkably uncomplicated causes.

A combination of easy money, instability of credit, and overinflated

---

[62] Lastra, R.M. (2009) *Northern Rock and Banking Law reform in the UK* in Bruni, F and D.T. Llewllyn (Eds) (2009) *The Failure of Northern Rock: A Multi-Dimensional Case Study* 131 – 156, Vienna: SUERF – The European Money and Finance Forum

[63]http://business.timesonline.co.uk/tol/business/industry_sectors/banking_and_finance/article3613804.ece

asset prices are present in both cases. None of these should come as a surprise, and nor are they unique. Other asset bubbles such as the Panic of 1857,[64] and the Stock Market Crash of 1987 have the exact same origin. In this respect Minsky argues that stability is instability, basically stating that long and unusual periods of economic stability generally result in an environment in which investors tend to take more risk, increase their borrowing and overpay for assets[65]. Fisher held a similar view and stated that although over-investment and over-speculation generally play an important role, the impact is magnified by the use of borrowed money[66].

In addition, the fact that the regulators have a tendency to focus on long-term stability of the banking industry and not on potential short-term liquidity crises renders the regulatory environment ineffective.

7.2 The Responses

"I can calculate the motion of heavenly bodies, but not the madness of people"
Sir Isaac Newton on the South Sea Bubble

After he allegedly lost £20,000[67] in the South Sea Bubble, Sir Isaac Newton despaired that he could not calculate the madness of people. He should have known better since he invented the mathematics that could prove the impossibility returns that were promised by the South Sea Company to an everlasting stream of new investors[68]. Here too, instability in the supply of credit was a major factor influencing both the boom and the bust. Sections 7.2.1 to 7.2.3 below focus on the

---

[64] Calomiris, C.W. and L. Schweikart (1991) *The Panic of 1857: Origins, Transmission, and Containment* The Journal of Economic History, Vol. 51, No. 4 807-834

[65] Kindleberger and Aliber (2005)

[66] Fisher, I (1933) *The Debt-Deflation Theory of Great Depressions* Econometrica Vol. 1, No. 4 337-357

[67] Equates to roughly £3m in today's money using the retail price index. www.measuringworth.com/ppoweruk

[68] Levenson, T (2009) *Even a Genius can get suckered*
http://articles.cnn.com/2009-07-29/politics/levenson.finance.regulation_1_markets-rational-bubble?_s=PM:POLITICS

responses by the general public, politicians and regulators during crises in general and the Great Depression and the Credit Crunch in particular.

7.2.1 The Public

Schyt Actien en Wind Handel

(Shit shares and swindle) – Dutch Market South Sea Bubble Plate ca 1725

Price movements on exchanges are to a considerable extent dependent on the mental attitude of the investing and trading public[69]. Responses to asset bubbles and their subsequent busts are generally emotive, as demonstrated by newspaper headlines and other expressions such as the playful Delft Blue earthenware plates dating from around 1725, and the rumours circulating after the 1929 Stock Market Crash related to an increase in suicide rates among financiers and investors. Fortunately, the latter appear largely unsubstantiated[70].

Behavioural finance is based around the concept of bounded rationality which recognises that people do not base all their decisions on facts but are influenced by other elements such as media. The human mind is limited in its capacity to what it can understand, especially when confronted with increased complexity. Investment decisions have to be made in a relatively short time and investors are strongly influenced by the perceived quality of a news source. Decisions are thus not fully

---

[69] Selden, G. C., (1912) Psychology of the Stock Market: Human Impulses Lead To Speculative Disasters. New York: Ticker Publishing.

[70] Galbraith, J.K (1955) *The Great Crash 1929* London: Hamish Hamilton

thought through and people are only rational within limits[71].

Public news releases such as changes in unemployment levels and the consumer price index strongly influence the investor's decision-making process and can have a significant impact on the price of securities, although generally only when the results are not as expected[72]. The responses of market participants are not restricted to macroeconomic news. As discussed in Chapter 6, there is the example from 1996, when Allan Greenspan, then chairman of the Federal Reserve Board, used the phrase *irrational exuberance* to describe the behaviour of stock market investors in a televised speech in Washington[73]. Immediately thereafter stock markets globally exhibited pride drops without any apparent reason[74]. Since then, the term has been used to characterise the social phenomenon that occurs when markets have been bid up to unusually high and unsustainable levels under the influence of a naïve and optimistic market psychology[75]. Unfortunately human behaviour is not something that can be regulated.

The sharp drop in share prices during the Stock Market Crash in 1929 and the Credit Crunch in 2008 were, at least in part, a correction for earlier *irrational exuberance*. In each case, considerable numbers of shares were overvalued and a market correction was at that point long overdue, although this is not the only explanation. The initial news surrounding Lehman's bankruptcy, for example, caused investors to sell

---

[71] Simon, H. (1957). *Models of Man, Social and Rational: Mathematical Essays on Rational Human Behavior in a Social Setting.* New York: Wiley.

[72] Balduzzi, P., J.E. Elton and T.C. Green (2001) *Economic News and Bond Prices: Evidence from the U.S. Treasury Market*, Journal of Financial and Quantitative Analysis, Vol. 36, No. 4, 523 – 543 Seattle: University of Washington School of Business Administration

[73] Greenspan, A. (1996) *The Challenge of Central Banking in a Democratic Society,* speech before the American Enterprise Institute for Public Policy, Washington, 5th December 1996

[74] See section 6.2

[75] Schiller, R.J. (2005) *Irrational Exuberance* second edition, Princeton, New Jersey: Princeton University Press

banking shares at heavily discounted prices. Lack of transparency, increasing complexity in financial instruments, and ambiguity about who was exposed to the credit risk on securitised financial assets, caused a situation in which the extent of the losses that were sustained did not become clear until much later, adding further uncertainty. The response from investors may perhaps have been excessive or even irrational, but the severity of their responses was not completely unexpected, particularly taking into consideration herd behaviour and reliance on certain news sources that are deemed to be reliable. Herd behaviour is not necessarily irrational, especially when the investor is trading on someone else's behalf. Investors are typically unwilling to take a contrary position since getting it wrong can have severe adverse consequences[76].

The collective memory is, however, fairly short. As mentioned previously, long and unusual periods of economic stability generally result in an environment in which investors take more risk, increase their borrowing and tend to over pay for assets[77]. Equally, many younger bankers, not having consciously lived through a crisis before, have been heard to comment that "this has never happened before", and "the financial world as we know it has come to an end"[78].

The public's response can easily be summarised as a combination of overconfidence in the build up and panic selling in the wake of the bursting of the bubble. Not only in the current crisis but equally in 1929, 1987[79], and any other asset bubble in history.

---

[76]Schoon (2009)

[77]Kindleberger and Aliber (2005)

[78]From a number of private conversations between the author and market participants.

[79] Wigmore, B.A. (1998) *Revisiting the October 1987 Crash* Financial Analysts Journal, Vol. 54, No. 1 p 36-48 Charlottesville: Association for Investment Management and Research

7.2.2 The Politicians

During the 1929 Stock Market Crash and the 2008 Credit Crunch, most politicians and government advisors were, prior to the bubble bursting, convinced that this time it really was going to be different. Some have stuck with their vision, others actively started to look at resolving matters, and yet another group was concerned with apportioning blame.

A few days before Black Thursday on the 24th of October 1929, Irving Fisher, a respected economist, stated that *"Stock prices have reached what looks like a permanently high plateau"*, which was followed by his observation on the 21st of October that the market was *"only shaking out of the lunatic fringe"*, which implied he felt that prices had still not caught up with their real value and should go much higher. As late as the 23rd of October 1929, one day before the crash, he even stated that *"security values in most instances were not inflated"*. Fisher stood by his observations which eventually caused him to lose all his assets[80]. Andrew Mellon, Secretary of the Treasury has been quoted to say in September 1929 that *"there is no cause to worry. The high tide of prosperity will continue"*. On 14th of October in the same year, Secretary Lamont and officials from the Commerce Department *"denied rumors that a severe depression in business and industrial activity was impending, which had been based on a mistaken interpretation of a review of industrial and credit conditions issued earlier in the day by the Federal Reserve Board."*[81]

More recently, in June 2007, Gordon Brown, in his last speech as Chancellor of the Exchequer of the United Kingdom, congratulated the City of London on its remarkable achievements and *"an era that history will record as the beginning of a new golden age"*[82].

---

[80] www.economist.com/node/13104022

[81] New York Times, 14 October 1929

[82] Speech by the Chancellor of the Exchequer, the Rt Hon Gordon Brown MP, to Mansion House. www.hm-treasury.gov.uk/press_68_07.htm

After the Stock Market Crash of 1929, turns of phrase such as *"orgy of speculation"* and *"we shall hear considerably less in the future of those newly invented conceptions of finance which revised the principles of political economy with a view solely to fitting the stock market's vagaries"*[83] were voiced and the general observation was that the Stock Market Crash was solely the result of speculation. Senator Frazier, for example, blamed the Federal Reserve Banks for diverting funds to *"Wall Street interests to gamble in stocks and bonds"*, and Professor Haney stated that the use of bank credit for speculative activities limited the supply of credit for genuine business activities[84]. With the benefit of hindsight and reflection, the view became more balanced with one of the reasons for the Stock Market Crash being cited as a failure of policies[85].

In the wake of the 2008 Credit Crunch politicians and the general public initially appear to have blamed the crisis mainly on the greed of the bankers[86], although there is an increasing realisation that regulatory and policy failures may have played a large role. Given time, however, it is expected that the emotional responses will give way to a more balanced analytical view. In ten years time, and with the benefit of hindsight, it is highly likely that the general responses to the current crisis are viewed as being similar to those of the 1929 Stock Market Crash.

Although a lot of emphasis has been placed on banker's remuneration,

---

[83] New York Times Editorial, 26 October 1929

[84] Eiteman, J.W. (1932) *The Economics of Brokers' Loans* The American Economic Review, Vol. 22, No. 1, 66-77

[85] Statement by Alan Greenspan Chairman Board of Governors of the Federal Reserve System before the Joint Economic Committee, United States Congress, June 17 1999.

[86] This is particularly clear from the MPs responses and line of questioning during the interview with Bob Diamond and Antony Jenkins for the HOC Treasury Committee. www.parliamentlive.tv/Main/Player.aspx?meetingId=7376

It is worth noting that it is painfully clear from the questions and attitudes that most of the MPs do not grasp the basics of finance and economics.

global market practice and the requirement to strike the balance between a motivational element and a potentially higher risk attitude that may result in a short-term attitude need to be considered. The making of bonuses contingent on continuing performance which banks and regulators have started to explore and implement since circa 2005 is likely to reduce excessive short-termism and risk taking. Such policies will have to be implemented globally in order to ensure that there will not be a human capital flight from one jurisdiction to another.

7.2.3 The Regulators

In February 1929 the Federal Reserve Board held the view that the high interest rates and tight money supply were evidence that the stock exchange absorbed significant amounts of available credit. This view was not shared by others such as Keynes, who stated that:

> "The high market rate of interest which prior to the collapse the Federal reserve system, in their effort to control the enthusiasm of the speculative crowd [...] played an essential part in bringing about the rapid collapse. For this punitive rate of interest could not be prevented from having its repercussions on the rate of new investment, both in the United States and throughout the world, and was bound, therefore, to prelude an era of falling prices and business losses everywhere." [87]

Hardy[88] points out that, by that time, the Federal Reserve's policy had been to increase the interest rate for at least a year. Since the influence of speculation on the market did not become evident until after their operations began, this played an instrumental role in the boom.

After the Stock Market Crash of 1929, one of the main actions was the reconstruction of the financial structure which was eventually put in place in 1936 and was based on two principles: compartmentalisation,

---

[87] Keynes, J.M. (1930) Treatise on Money, Volume II, The Applied Theory of Money London: Macmillan, p 196

[88] Hardy, C.O. (1937) *Recent Developments in the Theory of Speculations* The American Economic Review, Vol. 27, No. 1 Supplement, Papers and Proceedings of the 49th Annual Meeting of the American Economic Association, pp. 263-273

and transparency[89]. The Glass-Steagall Act of 1933 prohibited commercial banks from collaborating with full-service brokerage firms or participating in investment banking activities effectively resulting in compartmentalisation of the banking system. Over time a number of amendments were made to the Act[90] which was eventually repealed in 1999. In addition, the Securities Exchange Acts of 1933 and 1934 were passed, the main features of which were the establishment of the Securities and Exchange Committee (SEC) and the regulation of margin buying by introducing specific guidelines for the maximum credit that may be extended on a security[91].

The relative swiftness with which changes were made to the regulatory infrastructure after the Stock Market Crash of 1929 shows the perceived severity of the crisis. Similarly, the responses from the regulators to the 2008 Credit Crunch have been relatively swift with new regulations – Basel III[92] – being defined by the Basel Committee of Banking Supervision which are due to be implemented during 2012 - 2019. Although initially only applicable to G10 countries, the Basel guidelines have become the *de facto* guideline in most jurisdictions. Interestingly enough, many of the rules and guidelines included in Basel III were originally part of the Basel II proposals but were removed under political pressure.

In addition to the global standards outlined in the subsequent Basel Accords, flaws in the regulatory environments in individual jurisdictions have been identified. For the UK for example, a number of institutional weaknesses in the regulatory regime have been identified including a

---

89 Minsky (1993)

90 Heffernan, S.A. (1996) *Modern Banking in Theory and Practice* New York: John Wiley & Sons Inc p 238

91 T.J.F. (1934) *An Explanation of Fundamentals of Stock Market Practice and Procedure in Light f the Securities Exchange Act of 1934,* Virginia Law Review, Vol. 21, No. 1 103-111

92 BCBS (2010) *Basel III: A global regulatory framework for more resilient banks and banking systems*

fundamental flaw in the deposit protection scheme; the absence of a bankruptcy regime for banks; the absence of a well-established or predictable regime for handling troubled banks; and an institutional structure of financial supervision that separates the responsibility for systemic stability and lender of last resort (Bank of England) from prudential supervision (Financial Services Authority)[93]. The segregation of the lender of last resort function and the prudential supervision function is particular dangerous in crisis situations, and is being addressed by bringing supervision and regulation back under the sole responsibility of the Bank of England[94]. In addition, the interim report of the Independent Banking Commission (ICB)[95,96] addresses the issue of compartmentalisation of retail and wholesale banking which, incidentally, is similar to the aim of the Glass-Steagall Act of 1933 in the US which has since been repealed.

In the United States the Dodd-Frank Act – also known as the Financial Stability Act of 2010 – has been passed which deals, among others, with increased capital requirements, minimum lending standards, financial protection, and FDIC deposit protection[97]. Unlike the Basel III rules which introduce a 30-Day Liquidity Coverage Ratio and the Net Stable

---

[93] Llewellyn, D.T. (2009) *The Failure of Northern Rock: A Multi-Dimensional Case Study* in Bruni, F and D.T. Llewllyn (Eds) (2009) *The Failure of Northern Rock: A Multi-Dimensional Case Study* 13 – 34, Vienna: SUERF – The European Money and Finance Forum

[94] HM Treasury (2010) *A New Approach to Financial Regulation: Judgment, Focus and Stability* www.hm-treasury.gov.uk/d/consult_financial_regulation_condoc.pdf

[95] Independent Commission on Banking (2011) *Interim Report, Consultation on Reform Options* http://s3-eu-west-1.amazonaws.com/htcdn/Interim-Report-110411.pdf

[96] http://ftalphaville.ft.com/blog/2011/04/11/542021/how-to-ring-fence-a-tbtf/

[97] Brief Summary of the Dodd-Frank Wall Street Reform and Consumer Protection Act (2010) *Create a Sound Economic Foundation to Grow Jobs, Protect Consumers, Rein in Wall Street and Big Bonuses, End Bailouts and Too Big to Fail, Prevent Another Financial Crisis.* The Dodd-Frank Act is also known as the "Financial Stability Act of 2010"
http://banking.senate.gov/public/_files/070110_Dodd_Frank_Wall_Street_Reform_comprehensive_summary_Final.pdf

Funding Ratio to regulate for potential short-term liquidity disruptions[98], the Dodd-Frank Act does not regulate for the risk associated with the significant levels of short-term debt[99]. Under the new regulations considered in Europe which are based on the Basel III Accord, the proposed capital requirements considered are higher than those in the United States. Under political and industry pressure the regulations are, however, expected to converge to the less stringent version – in this case the US proposals with its lower capital requirements[100].

Whether these guidelines will be in force for long, whether they will be sufficient, or perhaps overshooting the mark will remain to be seen. The implementations of the Basel I Accord in 1988 and the introduction of Continuous Linked Settlements (CLS) in 2002 may provide some insight. Although long forgotten, both were a direct result of the bankruptcy of Herstatt Bank in 1974 and, particularly for the Basel Accord, it may have been a question of too little too late.

7.3 Lessons Learned

"History does not repeat itself, but it does rhyme"
Mark Twain

Asset bubbles and the inevitable financial crises that follow are not a modern phenomenon, but have been around since Tulip Mania in 1624 – 1637, and probably even before that. Unjustifiable increases in asset prices followed by the implosion of the bubble have potentially disastrous and far reaching consequences. With increased globalisation and the effects of contagion, the aftermath of financial crises is no longer restricted to relatively small groups or single jurisdictions but

---

[98] BCBS (2010)

[99] Acharya, V.V., T. Cooley, M. Richardson and I. Walter (2009) *Market Failures and Regulatory Failures: Lessons from Past and Present Financial Crisis* First Draft. Forthcoming in Kawai, M., E. S. Prasad *Financial Sector Regulation and Reforms in Emerging Markets* Washington DC: Brookings Institution Press

[100] www.ft.com/cms/s/0/5a31d69c-6460-11e0-a69a-00144feab49a.html

tend to spread regionally and even globally.

The two main financial crises reviewed in this section, the Stock Market Crash of 1929 and the 2008 Credit Crunch exhibit similar underlying circumstances. The expansion of relatively cheap credit, inflated asset prices, and the notion that this time it would all be different formed the basis for each of the asset bubbles. Equally, the bursting of bubbles is generally caused by one of two main reasons: the shifting balance of demand and supply and, more importantly, the instability of the supply of credit and the subsequent panic selling of assets for which there are no longer any buyers available.

The responses to crises differ based on the circumstances, but are typically at least in part fuelled by panic. When the news of Northern Rock's funding problems became public depositors panicked and wanted to withdraw all their funds from the bank, even after the Government guaranteed its stability.

Price movements associated with asset bubbles are generally not just caused by the underlying value of the asset but are, for a considerable part, dependent on the attitude of the investing and trading public. Responses to asset bubbles and subsequent busts tend to be emotive, often reinforced by sensationalist newspaper headlines. As the concept of bounded rationality shows, investment decisions are not solely based on facts but are influenced by other elements such as media and messages from politicians. Limitations of the human mind to deal with increased complexity and the generally limited time available to reach an investment decision often result in irrational decisions which are not fully thought through.

The responses of politicians tend to echo those of the general public, and are generally euphoric in times when prices are up. In the immediate aftermath of the Stock Market Crash of 1929, some remarks were made about the foolishness of investors, but attention was later turned to resolving the issues underpinning the crisis and the implementation of a wide range of measures. In the wake of the banking crisis of 2008, the current state of mind is still much one of apportioning blame, although this is likely to change as emotional responses will make way to more analytical reviews.

Both crises resulted in the implementation of additional regulation, some likely to be more effective than others. The Glass-Steagall Act of 1933, which ensured the compartmentalisation of banks and enhanced protection of depositors, was eventually repealed in 1999 and replaced by new legislation, significantly loosening the original requirements. The Securities and Exchange Acts of 1933 and 1934 have been amended over time, but are still largely in place. The current crisis has resulted in new legislation to be implemented in, for example, the United Kingdom and the United States as well as the development of global regulations in the form of the Basel III Accord.

If there is anything to be learned from asset price fuelled booms and busts it is that history does have a tendency to repeat itself. Instability of credit supply is difficult to regulate, largely because it is strongly correlated with trust between the market participants. As soon as the trust falls away all market participants tend to overreact, the consequences of which are panic sales and significant falls of asset prices. Changes in financial regulation always initially appear to resolve some of the associated issues, but are often amended and repealed over time. Unlike the American regulatory changes which largely ignore the issue of banks relying on short term liquidity, the Basel III Accord attempts to regulate for potential short-term liquidity disruptions with the introduction of the Liquidity Coverage Ratio and the Net Stable Funding Ratio. However, the Basel III guidelines allow for national discretion to be applied and it will remain to be seen how these measures will be implemented in different jurisdictions. In the US, regulation for short-term liquidity crisis is still not included in the regulations. The discrepancies that thus occur are likely to result in what is known as 'regulatory arbitrage' which, for large international banks, is relatively easy to implement.

What becomes painfully clear when comparing the different financial crises is that we collectively don't learn from the past. When times are good politicians, regulators and the general public alike, like the banks to make higher profits because of its positive impact on the overall economy. The higher risk levels required for this are easily overlooked as greed and a false sense of security take hold. Inevitably the bubble bursts and panic selling and blame apportionment ensue in combination with what can only be described as knee-jerk reactions from politicians and regulators. New policies and regulations are devised and, after many iterations, implemented. Differences between the regulations proposed in the US and those in the new Basel III Accord that will be applied in Europe and other jurisdictions will be tightened under pressure from the banks and politicians. After prolonged periods of economic stability the regulatory guidelines will be loosened.

Going forward, there are three main considerations for the global financial industry:

1. due to the fact that international financial markets are highly correlated, regulations should be agreed globally and not locally;
2. regulatory bodies should be truly independent and prevent any loosening of regulations when times are prosperous; and
3. the fact that regulators have a tendency to focus on long-term stability of the banking industry and to overlook the potential impact short-term liquidity crises, renders the regulatory environment ineffective.

Stringent regulations were introduced as the result of the 1930s crisis which were loosened over time under pressure of lobbyists and political calls for deregulation inevitably leading to the next asset bubble. As a result of the 2008 crisis, new regulations are being implemented. Only time will tell whether there will be a new crisis. Will history repeat itself or will it merely rhyme?

8 The History of the Prohibition of Interest

"The most powerful force in the universe is compound interest"
Albert Einstein

As a result of the growth of Islamic financial services, the prohibition of interest has gained renewed attention. Contrary to popular belief, however, the ban on interest is not unique to Islamic finance and has a long history going back at least as far as the Code of Hammurabi. Through the ages, interest has been a controversial subject and has been extensively debated by philosophers and theologians. In practice, however, it was common to charge a fee for money or goods lent – often by finding ways to circumvent legal restrictions on interest such as partnership and trade transactions. This section reviews the prohibition of interest over time from the Babylonians via the Greeks and the Romans to the anti-usury laws of the United Kingdom and the United States.

Evidence exists that as early as the 18th century BC priests in Babylon acted as money lenders to the merchants, and the Code of Hammurabi, believed to be the first codified law which was written around 1760 BC, includes laws governing banking operations in ancient Mesopotamia. It was a comprehensive set of laws which, although essentially humanitarian in intent and orientation, also contained concepts associated with behaviour such as corporate responsibility[101]. In addition, rules regarding repayment of debt, and permissible levels of payments for storage, safekeeping, and the amount of rent to be paid for obtaining the legal right to use and derive profit or benefit from property such as land and different species of livestock belonging to another were clearly defined. Article 93 of the code has been quoted to state that compound interest is not permissible[102], but although not

---

[101] King, L.W (2004), *The code of Hammurabi*, Kessinger Publishing.

[102] Saleh, N.A. (1986) *Unlawful gain and legitimate profit in Islamic law* Cambridge: Cambridge University

unlikely, most other sources refer to this article as being illegible.

The Ancient Greeks and Ancient Romans used to freely charge interest and generally secured both the debt and the interest on the borrower, as a result of which the borrower would automatically become the slave of the creditor in the event of default. King Bocchoriss (Egyptian 24th Dynasty (730 – 715 BC)) went as far as to forbid all taking of interest in excess of the principal[103].

During the 4th century BC, Aristotle, building further on the works of earlier philosophers, argued that although money was intended to be used in exchange, it was meant to be consumed, and could therefore not increase and does not have an intrinsic value of its own since it is merely a human social invention with no utility in itself[104]. In addition, he specifically defines the term usury as "the birth of money from money" which he rejected as the most unnatural way of making money since money does not have any self replicating properties.

At that point in time, the Jewish money lender was already long established, a situation that in part occurred due to the difference in interpretation of Deuteronomy 23:21 between Judaism and Christianity. Where Christians were not allowed to lend at interest to any human, Jews were only banned from lending at interest to a fellow Jew. They could, however, freely charge and pay interest to anyone gentile or, in other words, any non-Jew.

The Romans recognised the right to lend and borrow against a specified return, but did not permit excess returns on the *mutuum*, loans of money, oil, or other fungible goods. The *mutuum* were only permitted as long as the same kind and quality was returned to the lender, since fungible goods could not be separated from the substance and their

---

[103] Saleh (1986)

[104] Aristotle *The Politics* in Monroe (1948) *Early Economic Thought, selections from economic literature prior to Adam Smith*, Cambridge: Harvard University Press, 1-30

main purpose was to be consumed[105]. Fungible goods were defined as those that could be weighed, measured, or numbered[106]. In addition, interest was prohibited unless it was contractually agreed between the parties up front. The one contract in which interest was permitted was the *foenus nauticum,* a contract to lend money for large projects.

Roman law embodied in the *Lex Unicaria* of 88 BC recognised an interest rate of up to 12 per cent, which became the legal maximum in 50 BC by decree of the Senate. This decree remained in place until Justinian introduced a tiered structure in 533 AD in which 12 per cent was the legal maximum that could be charged for *foenus nauticum;* 8 per cent for business loans; 6 per cent for those not in business; and 4 per cent for distinguished persons and farmers[107]. Although it is unclear how the different rates were determined, it is likely that consideration had been given to the perceived risk associated with the transaction as well as the economic necessity of the loan.

With the demise of the Roman Empire from the late 4th century AD onwards and the subsequent development of the European nation states, the individual countries over time developed their own laws. In the initial stages, the Canon laws of the Church would generally be the leading body of law, but as time went on, they developed into a separate body of law. In the United Kingdom this process took place by means of a series royal decrees and later on acts of parliament.

The "Laws of Edward the Confessor", a compilation of 39 laws, dealt with Jewish as well as Christian usury and evidence exists that Henry II actively prohibited Christian usury as early as 1136[108].

---

[105] Jones, N. (2008) Usury, EH.Net Encyclopedia, edited by Robert Whaples, February 10, 2008. http://eh.net/encyclopedia/article/jones.usury

[106] Roover, R. De (1967) *The Scholastics, Usury, and Foreign Exchange,* Business History Review, Vol. 41, No. 3, 257-271

[107] Jones (2008)

[108] Seabourne, G. (2003) *Royal Regulation of Loans and Sales in Medieval England – Monkish Superstition and Civil Tyranny* Woodbridge: The Boydell Press

The Code of Canon Law from around 1187 clearly states that as far as the Church is concerned, the basic definition of usury is that it is everything that is asked in return for a loan, beyond the value of the loan itself. In itself, the earning of money through usury is deemed to be a sin forbidden by both the Old and the New Testament, as is just hoping to receive additional property beyond the property itself. Requesting a higher price for a sale on credit is also seen as an act of usury, albeit an implicit one. The Code further states that all gain acquired through usury must be reimbursed in full to the true owner[109]. Around the same time, Innocent III argued that no interest could be charged to Crusaders, but for all others, moderate interest was acceptable and Christians should only be protected against immoderate or excessive usury. Innocent III's decree specifically refers to the Jewish money lenders, implying that the charging and paying of interest between Christians was still not permissible[110].

In 1215, King John of England signed the first version of the Magna Carta which included two clauses dealing with any loans at interest that might be outstanding on the borrower's death. Neither of the clauses, however, made it into any of the subsequent versions[111].

---

[109] Goff, J. Le (1990) *Your Money or Your Life – Economy and Religion in the Middle Ages*, New York: Zone Books

[110] Stow, K.R. (1981) *Papal and Royal Attitudes toward Jewish Lending in the Thirteenth Century*, AJS Review, Vol. 6 161-184, Cambridge: Cambridge University Press on behalf of the Association for Jewish Studies

[111] If anyone who has borrowed a sum of money from Jews dies before the debt has been repaid, his heir shall pay no interest on the debt for so long as he remains under age, irrespective of whom he holds his lands. If such a debt falls into the hands of the Crown, it will take nothing except the principal sum specified in the bond.

If a man dies owing money to Jews, his wife may have her dower and pay nothing towards the debt from it. If he leaves children that are under age, their needs may also be provided for on a scale appropriate to the size of his holding of lands. The debt is to be paid out of the residue, reserving the service due to his feudal lords. Debts owed to persons other than Jews are to be dealt with similarly.

Source: www.bl.uk/treasures/magnacarta/translation/mc_trans.html

At the same time, the Fourth Lateran Council, which was conducted by Pope Innocent III, prohibited Jews from taking oppressive and excessive interest from Christians, but allowed them to lend money at interest as long as the rates were deemed to be reasonable. The ban on Jewish interest was, therefore, not absolute.

During the middle of the 13th century AD, Thomas Aquinas and his contemporaries including Ibn Rushd (Averroes) further explored Aristotle's views on the charging of interest and considered charging money for something that has been consumed to be unlawful[112]. In this respect, Aquinas also refers back to the civil law of the time which states:

> "things which are consumed in use do not receive a usufruct, either according to natural reason or civil law, and that the senate did not create a usufruct in their case (for it could not), but a quasi usufruct"

They did not reject the idea that capital could be put to productive use and that anyone providing capital should be rewarded for making it available, but purely rejected the providing of a loan at interest without any economic purpose, or without the lender taking at least some form of risk[113].

In the years 1274, 1275, and 1290 Edward I issued proclamations and statutes against usury, strongly condemning any form of it. In 1290 he expelled all Jews from England on the pretext that they were money lenders and thus committing a criminal offence. Although the charging of interest was banned (and there is evidence that some royal action was taken against usury) the ban on usury, which carried a penalty of excommunication under Canon law, was hardly enforced under any of the Royal decrees. It was not until 1363 that the first usurers were

---

[112] St Thomas Aquinas *Summa Theologica* in Monroe (1948) *Early Economic Thought, selections from economic literature prior to Adam Smith*, Cambridge: Harvard University Press, 51-78

[113] Goff (1990)

finally taken to trial[114].

One of the main challenges has long been the fact that the term usury in itself was rather loosely defined as the excess return on something that was lent. It was therefore unclear whether late payment penalties or selling at inflated prices for payment at a later date would fall under the prohibition or not. In addition, different rules appear to have been applied to Jews and Christians regarding the permissibility of applying an addition charge when selling on credit. Jews would be allowed to charge an additional amount over and above the sale price but Christians, to the contrary, were not. Until 1290 Jewish usury was, within limits, generally accepted and it was allowed for them to make a profit on loans. Besides the ban of charging usury to minor heirs that is defined in clauses 10 and 11 of the 1215 version of the Magna Carta and reiterated in the 5th clause of the Statute of Merton in 1235/6, Jews could freely charge usury and were not hindered by the government. This is, for example, evidenced by a charter of Henry III to the University of Oxford which allows the Jews of Oxford to take up to 2 pence (2d) per Pound per week from the scholars of the University as long as the interest would not be compounded[115]. There were other limitations in place specifying the percentages that could be charged. The draft Statute of the Jewry (1284-6), for example, limited the interest the Jewish money lenders could charge to "no more than half a mark for a loan of 20 shillings (20s) or 8 pence (8s 8d) per year, and for 40s, one mark, or 17s 4d, 'and for more, more, and for less, less'". In addition, the period of the loan was limited to a maximum of three to four years[116]. For Christians, however, all profit over and above the principal was banned, a ban that extended to profits on credit sales. In the year 1363 rules were put in place to enable action against circumvention of the usury laws. These rules applied in London, but did not get

114 Seabourne (2003)

115 Seabourne (2003)

116 Seabourne (2003)

introduced in the laws until 1487. The rules were particularly aimed at the practice known as *chevisance* which consisted of entering into a combination of artificial sales transaction, one at a higher price for future payment and the resale of the same asset at a lower price for immediate payment thus facilitating a loan against interest[117].

During the period leading up to the introduction of the 1571 Bill against usury, money lenders were occasionally taken to court. Actions taken to reduce the practice of usury, however, were fairly inconsistent. During the first part of Edward I's reign (1272 – 1307) any instance of usury was actively investigated and punished accordingly, and he went as far as to evict all Jews when they continued to charge usury after the Statute of Jewry in 1275. Subsequent royal decrees tended to refer to canon rules, thus making the charging of usury more like a moral sin than a criminal offence. A special usury tribunal was instated by the Court in 1363, but very few cases were pursued. The cases that were tried in the tribunal did not tend to result in severe punishments; a situation that remained as long as the prohibition was in place. It cannot be ignored that the royal actions were, at least in part, driven by financial motivations. The court of Edward I, for example, benefitted financially when actions were taken against the Jews and the Italian merchant usurers, and when Edward III included an anti-usury article in 1341-3 this was at least in part driven by the fact that he needed funds to meet the cost of his war with France. Tempting as it might be to assume that anti-usury action was largely governed by a desire to enhance the financial position of the Crown, this is unlikely to have been the case. Only a few cases were taken to court and there is no evidence of widespread confiscation of funds by the Crown. It is therefore reasonable to believe that, for at least a significant part, any action taken to combat usury was related to the desire to eradicate wrongful conduct and to avoid any adverse economic consequences for the country. Moreover, the laws were mainly aimed at the Christian

---

[117] Seabourne (2003)

usurers and only marginally dealt with the Jews and the Italian merchants, which would lead to the conclusion that the bans were mainly motivated by religious principles[118]. Around the same time, in the Ottoman Empire, all economic activity was subject to principles and rules in the *Qur'an* and the *Sunnah*, which prohibit all charging of interest. In practice, however, interest rates as high as 50% have been recorded.

In 1468, Henry VII introduced a law which defined usury as something that occurred when anyone lent:

> "money to and for a tyme, taking for the same lone any thing more besides or above the money lente by wey of contracte of covenaunte at the tyme of the same lone, Savyng laufull penaltees for nounpament of the same money lent."

Although this definition prohibited the general charging of interest, it did allow lenders to charge penalties on default[119]. In 1546, Henry VIII repealed this act and replaced it with an act on usury in which it was declared that all interest in excess of 10 per cent usurious and thus unlawful. This act was subsequently repealed by Edward VI, who again prohibited all charging of interest. The act appears not to have had the desired effect of eradicating lending at interest. To the contrary, there is reason to believe that instead it increased the amount of lending and in addition resulted in higher percentages charged[120]. The latter is likely related to the fact that the money lender would need to be compensated for the higher risk he was taking as a result of the prohibition.

In 1571, a Bill against Usury was presented in the House of Commons, which after having been subject to some debate in the months before

---

[118] Seabourne (2003)

[119] Jones, N (1989) *God and The Money Lenders: Usury and the Law in Early Modern England* Oxford: Basil Blackwell Ltd

[120] Smith, A. (1881)

was eventually passed in May[121]. Law started to play a larger role in society, and the concepts of usury as defined by Aquinas, who viewed it mainly as a factual and contractual matter were redefined to make it a crime of intent[122]. As long as the money lender could prove that the interest charge was not intended to be usurious the loan and the interest charge would be permissible. The comments made in Parliament clearly identify that the Law itself did not prohibit usury, since the act of Edward VI was repealed by Elizabeth on the grounds that it

> "hath not done so much good as was hoped it should but rather the said vice of usury and especially by way of sale of wares and shifts of interest hath much more exceedingly abounded to the utter undoing of many gentlemen, merchants, occupiers and others."

Elizabeth not only revived the statute of Henry VIII, but also the maximum legal interest rate of 10 per cent which remained in place until 1624 when it was reduced to 8 per cent[123]. The maximum interest rate was subsequently reduced to 6 per cent soon after the Restoration with the introduction of an act of parliament called *"An Act for restraining the takeing of Excessive Usury"* simultaneously introducing a penalty of £20 and imprisonment[124]. In 1714 the legal maximum was reduced to 5 per cent where it remained until 1854[125].

The legally maximum interest rate was not intended to set the market rate of interest but appears to have been determined based on the rate

---

[121] Journal of the House of Commons: May 1571, *The Journals of all the Parliaments during the reign of Queen Elizabeth* (1682), pp. 180-190. www.british-history.ac.uk/report.aspx?compid=43685&strquery=wilson 1571 usury

[122] Jones, N (1989)

[123] Smith (1881)

[124] Charles II, 1660: An Act for restraining the takeing of Excessive Usury, *Statutes of the Realm: volume 5: 1628-80* (1819), pp. 236-237. www.british-history.ac.uk/report.aspx?compid=47261

[125] Horack, B.S. (1941) *A Survey of the General Usury Laws* Journal of Law & Contemporary Problems, Vol. 8, No. 1, 36-53

a borrower of good credit quality could obtain in the market. The main justification for the introduction and subsequent maintaining of a maximum level of interest was that it was in the interest of advancing trade relations and agriculture[126]. Eventually, the law on usury was repealed, although this did not happen at once, but in a number of steps including the removal of Bills of Exchange up to three months from the scope of the law by the Bank Charter Act of 1833. All usury laws in the United Kingdom were finally abolished in 1854[127].

The Statute of Usury of 1714, which limited the interest rate that could be charged in the United Kingdom to 5 per cent, is generally accepted to be the basis for all anti-usury legislation in the United States. Contrary to European countries, where usury laws were repealed between 1854 and 1867, usury laws in the United States largely remained in place. There were, however, differences in individual states in the implementation of the laws. In 1850, New York State amended the law so that the maximum rate of usury only applied to individuals and excluded corporations from using the Act on Usury to reduce the interest they were charged, an example that was followed by many other states. In 1867, Massachusetts fully repealed their usury law on the basis that a market rate of interest could not be fixed without due consideration for the duration of the loan, the amount, or any collateral provided[128]. Massachusetts has since reinstated their usury law and a legal maximum rate of 20 per cent is now in place[129]. On the 31st of March 1980, President Carter signed The Depository Institutions Deregulation and Monetary Control Act into law. The purpose of title two of this law, the Depository Institutions Deregulation Act, was to

---

[126] Smith (1881)

[127] Horack (1941)

[128] Horack (1941)

[129] Massachusetts Legislature, General Laws, Part IV – Crimes, Punishments and Proceedings in Criminal Cases, Title I – Crimes and Punishments, Chapter 271 – Crimes Against Public Policy, Section 49 – Criminal Usury www.malegislature.gov/Laws/GeneralLaws/PartIV/TitleI/Chapter271/Section49

"provide for an orderly phase-out and ultimate elimination of interest rate ceilings" effectively repealing the anti-usury laws at federal level[130]. Most individual states still, however, enforce a maximum interest rate although there are significant differences of treatment in each state. The determination of the exact maximum interest rate is not straightforward. District of Columbia, for example, limits the interest to 24 per cent, except for loans in excess of USD 1,000 which are not a mortgage, where the borrower is a not for profit corporation, the loan is made for business purposes, or for the acquisition of property as an investment. For any other loan no maximum applies[131]. Nevada, on the other hand, does not apply any limits to the interest rate that can be charged provided that it is contractually agreed between the parties[132]. Virginia has set the legal maximum rate of interest to 12 per cent and allows for certain exemptions such as payday loans for which no legal maximum is defined, and pawnbrokers who are subject to a maximum rate of 10 per cent per month on amounts up to USD 25, 7 per cent per month for loans between USD 25 and 100, and 5 per cent for amounts in excess of USD 100 provided the loans are secured by tangible personal property[133]. The state of Washington has set the maximum legal rate of interest to the higher of 12 per cent or 4 per cent above the average Treasury Bill rate over the previous 26 months. The rule applies to consumers only, and has a large number of exceptions such as lease and hire-purchase transactions, retail instalment transactions,

---

[130] Federal Reserve Bank of Boston (1980) Depository Institutions Deregulation and Monetary Control Act of 1980 – summary booklet: www.bos.frb.org/about/pubs/deposito.pdf

[131] D.C. Code §28-3301 - §28-3314. Title 28 Commercial Instruments and Transactions, Subtitle II Other Commercial Transactions, Chapter 33 Interest and Usury. http://dc.gov/DC/Government/Publication%20Files/Consumer/LawsDecember21/InterestandUsury.doc - 2010-12-30

[132] Nevada Revised Statues – Title 8, Commercial Instruments and Transactions. Chapter 99, Money of Account and Interest. www.leg.state.nv.us/nrs/

[133] Code of Virginia 6.2.300. http://leg1.state.va.us/cgi-bin/legp504.exe?000+cod+6.2-300

credit card debt, and deferred payment sales contracts[134]. The legal maximum rates vary significantly between states and, as of May 2011, range between 5 per cent over the Federal Discount Rate, which currently equates to a total of 5.75 per cent[135], and 36 per cent[136].

More recently, an Interest Rate Reduction Act was introduced to congress on the 19th of January 2011 which is designed to amend Section 107 of the Truth in Lending Act to introduce a maximum interest rate of 15 per cent[137]. In the current version of the Act no such restriction is in place[138].

So, the prohibition on interest is not a new phenomenon, but rather one that has been around for a long time. Even though it was recognised that a cost was associated with providing capital, the charging of interest in return for a loan was deemed to be disadvantageous for individuals as well as the economy. Even so, lending at interest has always taken place in practice. With the changes in the economy from largely agricultural to more urban, the advent of the Industrial Revolution and the separation of Church and State, philosophers started to revise their view on the charging of interest. Adam Smith, for example argued that the lowest rate of interest charged should be just above the level to compensate for occasional losses to which lending is generally exposed, thus recognising the credit risk the lender is exposed to, but not much else. Although he strongly believe that a maximum rate of interest should be fixed in such a way

---

[134] Revised Code of Washington (RCW), Chapter 19.52 RCW Interest – Usury http://apps.leg.wa.gov/RCW/default.aspx?cite=19.52

[135] The Federal Discount Rate is the rate at which an eligible financial institution can borrow from the Federal Reserve Bank. On 18 May 2011, the rate was 0.75% www.bankrate.com/rates/interest-rates/federal-discount-rate.aspx

[136] www.loanback.com/category/usury-laws-by-state/

[137] Congressional Bills 112th Congress, 1st Session. H.R. 336 Introduced in House. www.gpo.gov/fdsys/pkg/BILLS-112hr336ih/html/BILLS-112hr336ih.htm

[138] FDIC Law, Regulation and Related Acts, 15 U.S.C. 1606 www.fdic.gov/regulations/laws/rules/6500-200.html#fdic6500107

that it would be slightly in excess of the market rate on a good security, but not too much above since that would result in speculation[139].

Jeremy Bentham on the other hand, opined that there is no requirement for a legal maximum interest rate since interest should instead be based on free choice, negotiation between the parties, and demand and supply. The agreed rate of interest should, in his view, depend on the price someone is willing to pay for the use of money in a similar way as the price for any other asset is determined[140].

In the end, the ability to use capital has a cost associated with it, and interest is still the benchmark that allows for the pricing of cost of funds, risk, opportunity cost, and future growth.

---

[139] Smith (1881)

[140] Bentham, J (1787) *Defence of Usury; Shewing the Impolity of the Present Legal Restraints on the Terms of Pecuniary Bargains In a Series of Letters to a Friend To Which is Added A Letter to Adam Smith, Esq; LL.D. On the Discouragements opposed by the above Restraints to the Progress of Inventive Industry*

9 Concluding Remarks

This book has two distinct parts. Part 1 details how the fundamental value of banks can be estimated using a Residual Income based valuation model. Part 2 explores items such as behavioural finance, the impact of news and media, Value at Risk, asset bubbles, and the history of the prohibition of interest. These are important factors in accounting for variations in actual market value from valuation models.

9.1 The Model and Parameters

The Residual Income model applied in this book is not new, but is based on the model that has been extensively tested for non-financial firms and fine-tuned by Frankel and Lee.

The findings for conventional banks are based on panel data using analysis which shows that as long as the parameters of the model are estimated correctly, the estimated fundamental value explains a large percentage of cross-sectional variations in market prices. The parameters are determined as follows:

- *Earnings* is measured using Earned for Ordinary;
- *Capital* consists of share capital and reserves but excludes any deposits given to the bank since these are considered to be of an operational nature;
- *Risk* is measured by β and used to determine the required return on equity;
- *Growth* is based on the I/B/E/S consensus forecast; and
- *Book value* is represented by the reported book value.

The analysis was carried out using two samples, one to estimate the regression, and one control sample. Both samples contained an equal number of banks with the same ratio of US versus European banks and a similar population size. The results show a high correlation between the market price and the value estimated using the Residual Income model, controlled for first-degree serial autocorrelation and heteroskedasticity. The goodness of fit for the estimation sample is 80%, with a confidence level of 99%. The control sample is then used to measure how close the unrestricted estimates of the control sample come to the coefficient found in the estimation sample.

The results from the various analyses imply that more than 80% of the cross-sectional variation in stock prices can be explained by the estimated fundamental value calculated using the Residual Income Model, which is in line with the findings of Frankel and Lee who use the same model for non-financial industries. Based on the results of this study it can be concluded that the Residual Income model can be applied to banks, and it is established that there is a relationship between the accounting measure and the stock market measure. A significant percentage of the cross-sectional variations in stock market prices of conventional banks can be explained by the value of the firm calculated by the model.

9.2 VaR, Behaviour, Asset Bubbles, and Interest

Notwithstanding the fact that the model appears to be able to provide a realistic value of a bank, there are a number of additional items that may have an impact on how a bank is perceived.

9.2.1 Value at Risk

VaR, originally devised as a measure to report financial risks, has widely been used to attempt to measure the downside risk of either a portfolio or, in aggregation, a firm into one single number. It is a numbers-based methodology based on past patterns. The output of a VaR equation attempts to measure the downside risk taking into account financial leverage and diversification effects across all markets and instruments. It represents the maximum amount a bank is likely to stand to lose on a given day or over a number of days (e.g. over a period of one week), generally with a confidence interval of 95% or 99%.

Over time, banks started to use VaR as a risk control tool. Trading limits were complemented by VaR limits, and at a firm level it was used to control firm-wide risk-taking diversification. From an initially passive tool, it started to be developed into a tool for actively controlling risk and subsequently into a risk allocation tool. It is designed to incorporate traditional risks and risks related to adverse market movements of financial derivatives and structured products. In addition, VaR is often used as a basis to calculate the amount of economic capital required to support a business, which is an essential component of economic value added measures. However, when the markets crashed in 2008, it became painfully clear that VaR was not as robust as was always assumed. There is a lot to say against VaR. The use of short term historic data, the black swans, the fact that non-traded instruments are not included are all issues that may need to be addressed. However, it does provide a single number that is easy to understand. Although it may be flawed, it is still the best number out there when it comes to a firm's risk. Enhancing the VaR methodology by incorporating recognition of cyclicality and defaults and the inclusion of non-traded assets may potentially be an expensive exercise and could lead to other challenges. Attaching less individual importance to the VaR, thoroughly analysing trends, and use it in combination with other risk management tools such as, for instance, Risk Adjusted Return on Capital (RAROC) might provide a more rounded view on the risk a financial institution takes. After all, VaR does not consider what could happen in the other 1% of the time.

Risks taken by a bank will have to be evaluated against its risk management system, as well as the cost of the measures in place. The complexity of banks seriously hinders simple assessment of the risks taken and how they are controlled. It will never be possible to incorporate safeguards against all risks within the risk management system of a bank. Increasing complexity may increase cost, transparency and potentially creates a false sense of security.

9.2.2 Behavioural Finance

Valuation models generally assume that investors exhibit rational behaviour when they make their investment decisions. This is not necessarily the case. The human mind is not capable of understanding everything, particularly when dealing with increased complexity. In addition, people are generally influenced by news and the perceived quality of the source. As a result, decisions are not fully thought through and people can only be rational within limits. Not only macroeconomic news is relevant, but also investor radio and television programmes or even speeches as was shown by the unexplained drop in stock market prices on Allan Greenspan's mention of the term *irrational exuberance* to describe the behaviour of stock market investors.

The power of herd behaviour should not be underestimated. During the Credit Crunch, significant uncertainty and increased complexity caused investors to start selling, and resulted in a downward spiral. Herd behaviour is however not necessarily irrational. After all, no one wants to be seen as the one that went against common practice and to be the only one to have got it wrong.

9.2.3 Asset Bubbles

Financial crises generally follow a period of inflated asset prices also known as an asset bubble. The underlying asset typically exhibits an unjustifiably sharp increase in price mainly caused by a combination of excess demand and investor sentiment. During the build up of the asset bubble there is a collective belief in the sustainability of the value of the asset. The financial crisis that invariably follows is often the result of withdrawal of liquidity from the markets and the loss of trust between market participants. The responses from the public, regulators and politicians seem to follow a similar pattern, and additional regulation, some likely to be more effective than others, is typically introduced and, as time goes by, piece by piece withdrawn losing sight of the original intention.

When times are good politicians, regulators and the general public alike, are all in support of banks making higher profits, and the fact that this requires a higher risk is often ignored. When things turn sour, panic selling and blame apportionment follow. New policies and regulations are devised and, after much iteration, implemented, often when it is too late.

9.2.4 The Prohibition on Interest

The prohibition on interest has a long history going back at least as far as the Code of Hammurabi. Through the ages interest has been a controversial subject and has extensively been debated by philosophers and theologians. Laws have been in place for extensive periods of time, and are, in case of the US, still active. The view on charging of interest has changed over time from all interest to only excessive interest, which was reflected in the laws.

9.3 Capturing Bank Fundamental Value

In a semi-strong form efficient market, it is assumed that all publicly available information is immediately and fully reflected in the share price. Any profits from seeking out over- or undervalued stocks will only be available to investors with insider information. However, as the test results illustrate, it is possible to identify over- or under-valuation of a set of firms in an industry without access to insider information.

Over the past 15 years, the financial system has experienced a variety of booms and busts, some more severe than others. In each case, share prices have responded more strongly than the estimated fundamental values. The most recent financial crisis has caused more disturbance, however, than the previous Asian crisis and dot.com boom. This becomes clear from the difference in the panel data test results.

Period	Price explained by value
1993 – 2002	80.6%
1993 – 2008	78.5%

Table 5 – Proportion of price explained by fundamental value

During the first period, 1993 – 2002, in excess of 80% of the price was explained by the estimated fundamental value of the banks. In the period 1993 – 2008 this was reduced by more than 2%. Most of this difference can be ascribed to the development of prices during the period 2006 – 2008. The end of the current crisis is not yet in sight though, and only time will tell whether the results represented in table 9 above might be distorted only temporarily.

Other factors, such as herd behaviour, have been identified as potential contributors to the remaining 20% of banking sector share prices.

A brief look at the FTSE All-Share Index shows that, although the reactions of the index to economic crises appear much more severe than in the bank sample, the trend line is very similar across other sectors of the economy, as can be seen from Figure 6 below.

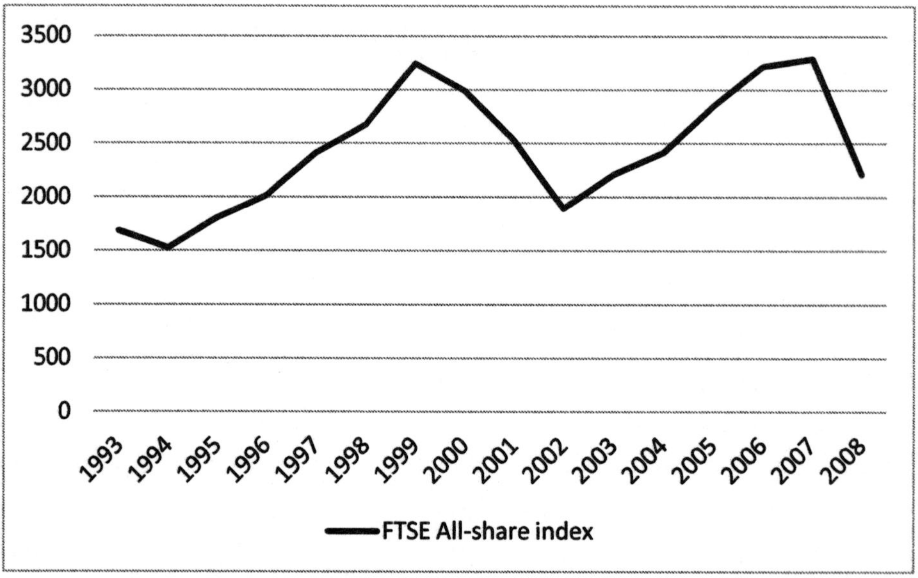

Figure 6 – FTSE All-Share Index 1993 - 2008

Determining the estimated fundamental value for the constituents of the index is well beyond the remit of this book, but the above illustrates how connected the global economy appears to be.

In uncertain times the goodness of fit of the Residual Income model used to estimate the fundamental value of the banks in the sample deteriorates slightly. However, the model identified is this study and described in detail in Chapter 2 generally holds up well, even in uncertain times. At the aggregated sample level, the estimated fundamental value can be used as a check to determine whether the share prices are inflated or depressed.

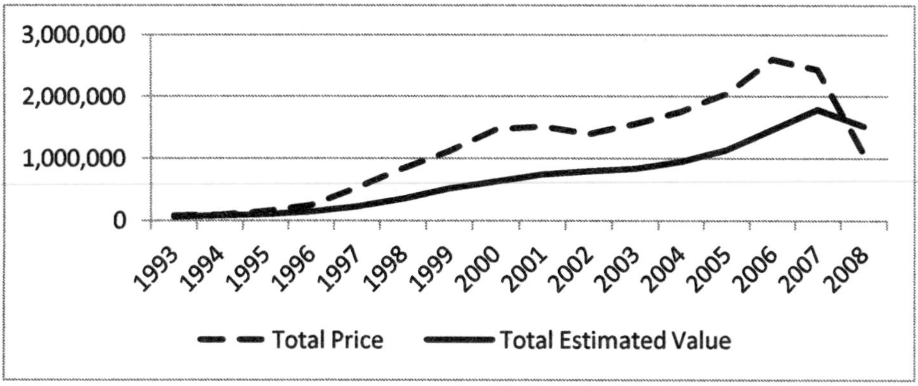

Figure 7 – Total price and total estimated fundamental value 1993 – 2008 (in $mn)

As illustrated by Figure 7 above, the spread between the estimated fundamental value and price widens and contracts over time. The fundamental value does however capture a significant part of the total price. It is not until 2008 that we see a significant adjustment of the price which is likely not solely caused by the estimated fundamental value but in part a consequence of the way investors have responded to the significant events that took place during the later period of the study. It is unfortunately too early to determine whether this might have been an overreaction.

The results for individual banks differ and are dependent on individual circumstances at the end of each period that is measured. Careful analysis of the individual banks gives an indication that the fundamental value estimated using the Residual Income model may enable the investor to seek out over- and undervalued banks. From the sample of 115 banks used for this research, a few interesting observations can be made:

- The general trend shows that, like the average, individual banks are generally overvalued, in some times quite significantly;
- Although there are exceptions, the US based banks tend to follow each other more closely than the European banks;
- A relatively higher proportion of European banks appears undervalued in the years 2003 and 2004, which could indicate that these banks have generally suffered more from the Asian crisis and the dot.com boom;
- Individual banks' market capitalisation is generally higher than the estimated fundamental value, and very few occasions of under-valuation are observed, although during the earlier period of the study one bank's market capitalisation was 25% of estimated fundamental value, and during the period 2003 – 2004, two of the banks market capitalisation was as low as 80% of estimated fundamental value. Banks are generally overvalued, and rarely undervalued. This is likely to be because of the perceived "safety" of bank shares.

Glossary

Term	Definition
APT	Arbitrage Pricing Theory
β	Beta – systematic, undiversifiable risk of an investment in comparison with the overall market
B^e_t	Book value of a firm per share at time *t*
CAPM	Capital Asset Pricing Model
CDO	Collateralised Debt Obligation
CML	Capital Market Line
CV	Continuing Value
DCF	Discounted Cash Flow
EPS	Earnings per Share
E-V	Expected Return – Variance
EVA	Economic Value Added
F1MN	I/B/E/S consensus growth forecast, 1 year forward
F2MN	I/B/E/S consensus growth forecast, 2 years forward
FCF	Free Cash Flow
g	Long-term sustainable growth rate
I/B/E/S	International Brokers' Estimated System. Collection of estimates for over 45,000 companies provided by 1,200 contributors
IAS	International Accounting Standard
LIBOR	London Interbank Offer Rate
LTCM	Long Term Capital Management

GLOSSARY

Term	Definition
LTMN	I/B/E/S consensus long-term growth expectation
OLS	Ordinary Least Squares
R^2	Goodness of Fit
RAROC	Risk Adjusted Return on Capital
r_e	Required return on equity
R_f	Risk-free rate of return
RI	Residual Income
R_m	Market rate of return
ROE	Return on Equity
SEC	Securities and Exchange Committee (US)
SML	Security Market Line
VaR	Value at Risk
V^e_t	Fundamental per share value of a firm estimated using a Residual Income Model at time *t*
WACC	Weighted Average Cost of Capital
X	Independent variable in the regression model
Y	Dependent variable in the regression model

Bibliography

Alpert, B (2009) *Cramer's Star Outshines his Stock Picks* and *The Cramer Effect – and Defect* (February 2007), www.smartmoney.com/investing.

Acharya, V.V., T. Cooley, M. Richardson and I. Walter (2009) *Market Failures and Regulatory Failures: Lessons from Past and Present Financial Crisis* First Draft. Forthcoming in Kawai, M., E. S. Prasad *Financial Sector Regulation and Reforms in Emerging Markets* Washington DC: Brookings Institution Press

Aquinas, T, *Summa Theologica* in Monroe (1948) *Early Economic Thought, selections from economic literature prior to Adam Smith*, Cambridge: Harvard University Press, 51-78

Aristotle, *The Politics* in Monroe (1948) *Early Economic Thought, selections from economic literature prior to Adam Smith*, Cambridge: Harvard University Press, 1-30

Balduzzi, P., J.E. Elton and T.C. Green (2001) *Economic News and Bond Prices: Evidence from the U.S. treasury Market*, Journal of Financial and Quantitative Analysis, Vol 36, No 4, 523 – 543 Seattle: University of Washington School of Business Administration

Barker, R. (2001) *Determining Value – Valuation Models and Financial Statements*, Harlow: Pearson Education Limited

BCBS (2010) *Basel III: A global regulatory framework for more resilient banks and banking systems*

Bentham, J (1787) *Defence of Usury; Shewing the Impolity of the Present Legal Restraints on the Terms of Pecuniary Bargains In a Series of Letters to a Friend To Which is Added A Letter to Adam Smith, Esq; LL.D. On the Discouragements opposed by the above Restraints to the Progress of Inventive Industry*

Bernstein, Peter L. (1998) *Against the Gods: The Remarkable Story of Risk* New York: John Wiley & Sons

Bierman, H (2010) *The 1929 Stock Market Crash* http://eh.net/encyclopedia/article/bierman.crash

Black, F. (1980) *The Magic in Earnings, Economic Earnings versus Accounting Earnings*, Financial Analysts Journal, 36 (November/December), 19-24

Brealey, R.A., S.C. Myers and A.J. Marcus (2003) *Fundamentals of Corporate Finance*, International Edition, New York: McGraw-Hill

BIBLIOGRAPHY

Brendon, P (2009) *With Bubbles, it's plus ça change...* Financial World, July/August 2009, London: CSFI

Calomiris, C.W. and L. Schweikart (1991) *The Panic of 1857: Origins, Transmission, and Containment* The Journal of Economic History, Vol. 51, No. 4 807-834

Centre for the Study of Financial Innovation (CSFI), 2009 *Grumpy Old Bankers: Wisdom from Crisis Past.* London: CSFI

Constantinides, G.M., Harris, M, Stulz, R.M, *Handbook of the Economics of Finance: Corporate Finance,* Amsterdam: Elsevier B.V.

Copeland, T.E, T. Koller and J. Murrin (2000) *Valuation: Measuring and Managing the Value of Companies,* 3rd Edition, New York: John Wiley & Sons

Copeland, T.E and J.F. Weston (1992) *Financial Theory and Corporate Policy* 3rd Edition, New York: Addison Wesley Publishing Company

Dash, M (1999) *Tulipomania* London: Victor Gollancz

Ederington, L. H., and J. H. Lee (1993) *How Markets Process Information: News Releases and Volatility* Journal of Finance, Vol 48, 1161-1191.

Eiteman, J.W. (1932) *The Economics of Brokers' Loans,* The American Economic Review, Vol. 22, No. 1, 66-77

Fama, E.F. (1970) *Efficient Capital Markets: A Review of Theory and Empirical Work,* The Journal of Finance, 25(2), 383-417

Fisher, I (1933) *The Debt-Deflation Theory of Great Depressions* Econometrica Vol. 1, No. 4 337-357

Frankel, R. and M.C. Lee (1998) *Accounting Valuation, Market Expectation, and Cross-sectional Stock Returns,* Journal of Accounting and Economics, 25, 283-319

Galbraith, J.K (1955) *The Great Crash 1929* London: Hamish Hamilton

Goff, J. Le (1990) *Your Money or Your Life – Economy and Religion in the Middle Ages,* New York: Zone Books

Greenspan, A. (1996) *The Challenge of Central Banking in a Democratic Society,* speech before the American Enterprise Institute for Public Policy, Washington, 5th December 1996

Gujarati, D.N. (2002) *Basic Econometrics,* 4th Edition, New York: McGraw-Hill International Editions

Hardy, C.O. (1937) *Recent Developments in the Theory of Speculations,* The American Economic Review, Vol. 27, No. 1 Supplement, Papers and Proceedings of the 49th Annual Meeting of the American Economic Association, pp. 263-273

Heffernan, S.A. (1996) *Modern Banking in Theory and Practice* New York: John Wiley & Sons Inc p 238

HM Treasury (2010) *A New Approach to Financial Regulation: Judgement, Focus and Stability*

Horack, B.S. (1941) *A Survey of the General Usury Laws Journal of Law & Contemporary Problems*, Vol. 8, No. 1, 36-53

Independent Commission on Banking (2011) *Interim Report, Consultation on Reform Options*

Jones, N (1989) *God and The Money Lenders: Usury and the Law in Early Modern England* Oxford: Basil Blackwell Ltd

Jones, N. (2008) *Usury*, EH.Net Encyclopedia, edited by Robert Whaples, February 10, 2008.

Keynes, J.M. (1930) *Treatise on Money, Volume II, The Applied Theory of Money,* London: Macmillan, p 196

Kimball, R.C. (1998) *Economic Profit and Performance Measurement in Banking*, Boston: New England Economic Review, July/August, 35-53

Kindleberger, C.P. and R.Z. Aliber (2005) *Manias, Panics and Crisis – A History of Financial Crises* New York: Palgrave Macmillan

King, L.W (2004), *The Code of Hammurabi*, Kessinger Publishing.

Lastra, R.M. (2009) *Northern Rock and Banking Law reform in the UK* in Bruni, F and D.T. Llewllyn (Eds) (2009) *The Failure of Northern Rock: A Multi-Dimensional Case Study* 131 – 156, Vienna: SUERF – The European Money and Finance Forum

Lee, C.M.C., J. Myers and B. Swaminathan (1999) *What is the Intrinsic Value of the Dow,* The Journal of Finance, 54(5), 1693-1741

Levenson, T (2009) *Even a Genius can get suckered* http://articles.cnn.com/2009-07-29/politics/levenson.finance.regulation_1_markets-rational-bubble?_s=PM:POLITICS

Llewellyn, D.T. (2009) *The Failure of Northern Rock: A Multi-Dimensional Case*

Study, in Bruni, F and D.T. Llewllyn (Eds) (2009) The Failure of Northern Rock: A Multi-Dimensional Case Study 13 – 34, Vienna: SUERF – The European Money and Finance Forum

Markowitz, H. (1952) *Portfolio Selection*, The Journal of Finance, 12(1), 77-91

Marshall, A. (1895) *Principles of Economics*, 3rd Edition, London: Macmillan & Co

McCulloch, H (1863) *Circular Letter of the Treasury Department, Office of the Comptroller of the Currency.* As quoted in Centre for the Study of Financial Innovation (CSFI), 2009 *Grumpy Old Bankers: Wisdom from Crisis Past.* London: CSFI

Milne, A. and G. Wood (2008), *Banking Crisis Solutions: Old and New Review,* Federal Reserve Bank of St Louis, September/October 2008, pp. 517–530.

Minsky, H.P. (1993) *Finance and Stability: The Limits of Capitalism* The Levy Economics Institute of Bard College, Working Paper number 93

Roache, Shaun K. and M. Rossi (2009) *The Effects of Economic News on Commodity Prices: Is Gold Just Another Commodity?* IMF Working Paper 09/140, Washington: IMF

Roover, R. De (1967) *The Scholastics, Usury, and Foreign Exchange,* Business History Review, Vol. 41, No. 3, 257-271

Saleh, N.A. (1986) *Unlawful gain and legitimate profit in Islamic law* Cambridge: Cambridge University

Schiller, R.J. (2005) *Irrational Exuberance* second edition, Princeton, New Jersey: Princeton University Press

Schoon, N (2009) *Valuing Banks in Uncertain Times* London: Spiramus Press

Seabourne, G. (2003) *Royal Regulation of Loans and Sales in Medieval England – Monkish Superstition and Civil Tyranny* Woodbridge: The Boydell Press

Selden, G. C., (1912) *Psychology of the Stock Market: Human Impulses Lead To Speculative Disasters.* New York: Ticker Publishing.

Shefrin, H (2002) *Beyond Greed and Fear: Understanding Behavioral Finance and the Psychology of Investing.* Oxford: Oxford University Press

Simon, H (1957). *Models of Man, Social and Rational: Mathematical Essays on Rational Human Behavior in a Social Setting.* New York: Wiley.

Smith, A. (1881) *An Inquiry into the Nature and Causes of the Wealth of Nations, Abridged version with notes and appendices by Wolsely P. Emerton, M.A. B.C.L.*, Oxford: James Thornton

Stow, K.R. (1981) *Papal and Royal Attitudes toward Jewish Lending in the Thirteenth Century*, AJS Review, Vol. 6 161-184, Cambridge: Cambridge University Press on behalf of the Association for Jewish Studies

T.J.F. (1934) *An Explanation of Fundamentals of Stock Market Practice and Procedure in Light of the Securities Exchange Act of 1934*, Virginia Law Review, Vol. 21, No. 1 103-111

Thomas, J.J. (1983) *An Introduction to Statistical Analysis for Economists*, London: London School of Economics Handbooks in Economic Analysis, 2nd edition;

Thompson, E.A. (2007), *The tulipmania: Fact or artifact?* Public Choice 130(1–2): 99–114.

Walker, M. (1997) *Clean Surplus Accounting Models and Market-based Accounting Research: A Review*, Accounting and Business Research, 27(4), 341-355

Wigmore, B.A. (1998) *Revisiting the October 1987 Crash*, Financial Analysts Journal, Vol. 54, No. 1 p 36-48 Charlottesville: Association for Investment Management and Research

Index